Everyone needs a pastor, but not everyone ha
He's a pastor who not only loves my family ar
contents of this book, loves God and His W
for a pastor to have a compassionate heart to
he doesn't have an understanding mind of Gc
heartedly recommend both the man and th

Green has spoken into my life as the pastoral covering to both my family and me. He has cared for my children, baptized my son-in-law, performed the marriage of my daughter, hand-held my wife and me through the "valley of the shadow," and taught me to fear no evil. He is a master guide who knows the road map well. The study of this book will open your eyes to the ancient secrets of another book—the Bible. I encourage you to pick this book up in one hand, your Bible in the other hand, and let Charles Green lead you to *The Revelation of God and His Word*.

—TOMMY TENNEY
AUTHOR OF *GODCHASERS*

Dr. Charles Green was the guest speaker at one of our annual pastor con-ferences and mentioned *The Revelation of God and His Word* study course and how much it had impacted his church leadership and congregation. At the time, I was searching for a course of study that would pull our church together in leading committed spirit-filled lives. As a senior pastor, I taught the foundational course during our Sunday morning worship services for a twenty-two-week period. The course helped us launch a renewal in the spiritual life of our people and has also led to the church's physical growth. Applying the basic principles and doctrines taught from *The Revelation of God and His Word* material, our church people have experienced a greater desire for change in their everyday lives. Dr. Green is a master teacher and expounder of God's Word, and it is revealed in the teachings contained in this life-anchoring work. I look forward to his authorship of this material and the great blessing it will be to the body of Christ.

—PASTOR JOHN STITT
RIVERSIDE CHURCH, NORMAN, OKLAHOMA

Dr. Charles Green is known around the globe as an exemplary pastor. After having passed to his son the mantle of Faith Church, the great local body he founded and pastored for a half-century in New Orleans, Louisiana, Dr. Green now teaches pastors worldwide. That ministry surprises no one who knows him, as Dr. Green has always been a dynamic teacher and an exqui-site wordsmith at relating the Word of God to people of all walks of life. This present work exemplifies Dr. Green's rare skill. As a former professor on the graduate faculty of a major northeastern university, an attorney, and novelist (whose decision to leave the professorship to return to Louisiana was partially based upon returning to Charles Green's spiritual pastoral guidance and teaching), I strongly recommend this work for those who desire to construct a rigid, faithful life-long biblical foundation in their lives. This work that Dr. Green has toiled over is suitable—no, it is a vital source—for all levels of teaching the doctrines and principles of God's Word from Genesis to Revelation for the new Christian and beyond.

—GLYN J. GODWIN, PhD, JD
AUTHOR OF BODY POLITIC

The Revelation of God and His Word is a genuine treasure. As a three-time student of the class using this book and a subsequent instructor using these materials, I am impressed with its ability to continue to teach in a fresh new way each time you approach it. If you want to build a strong foundation in godly things, this is the way to do it. Many of our students referred to this book as "Jesus 101." It goes in exciting speed from Adam and Abraham all the way to what's happening today. The availability of Teacher Notes for this material makes it even more valuable.

Charles Green is my beloved spiritual father. He has poured out his heart in these pages to enrich your life as he did in our classroom. Allow the author to embrace you with his godly love...nd be blessed.

—BERT R. BRATTON, MD

I have known Pastor Charles Green for over thirty years, and it is an honor for me to say that *The Revelation of God and His Word* is one of his landmark works. One of the amazing qualities of this book is its layers of information. For the new believer it is beautiful instruction on the Bible from Genesis to Revelation, and for the mature believer it reveals the hidden things of the Lord. I highly recommend this book to every Christian who is hungry.

—ROBERT KATZ
AUTHOR OF MONEY CAME BY THE HOUSE THE OTHER DAY AND
BIBLICAL ROADS TO FINANCIAL FREEDOM
PRESIDENT, KATZ, GALLAGHER COMPANY, CPA

It is so refreshing to hear a *father* explain foundational principles that I know he personally walks in. Every church should use this book to raise up the believers in their care. As an avid boat enthusiast well versed in navigation, I believe this is a GPS (global positioning signal) from God to his church to get us safely through all the religious debris and bring us into God's intended purpose for a glorious church. Thank you, Charles Green, my spiritual father, for a timely book.

—BISHOP BART PIERCE
ROCK CITY CHURCH
BALTIMORE, MARYLAND

THE
REVELATION
of GOD
and HIS
WORD

CHARLES GREEN

CREATION
HOUSE
A STRANG COMPANY

THE REVELATION OF GOD AND HIS WORD by Charles Green
Published by Creation House
A Strang Company
600 Rinehart Road
Lake Mary, Florida 32746
www.creationhouse.com

Unless otherwise noted, all Scripture quotations are from the New King James Version of the Bible. Copyright ©1979, 1980, 1982 by Thomas Nelson, Inc., publishers. Used by permission.

Scripture quotations marked KJV are from the King James Version of the Bible.

Scripture quotations marked AMP are from the Amplified Bible. Old Testament copyright © 1965, 1987 by the Zondervan Corporation. The Amplified New Testament copyright © 1954, 1958, 1987 by the Lockman Foundation. Used by permission.

Word definitions are derived from *Webster's Ninth New Collegiate Dictionary* (Springfield, MA: Merriam-Webster, Inc., 1985).

Hebrew and Greek definitions are derived from *Strong's Exhaustive Concordance of the Bible*, ed. James Strong (Nashville, TN: Thomas Nelson Publishers, 1997).

Cover design by Terry Clifton

Library of Congress Control Number: 2004117101

International Standard Book Number: 1-59185-783-X

Author's Note: The doctrinal points contained in this book are the opinions of the author, based upon what he considers to be Scriptural principles. Some of these, as in any book of this nature, might be controversial. The author does not claim—nor does he believe—that his doctrine is the only way to heaven. Jesus alone is the Way, the Truth, and the Life.

05 06 07 08 09 — 987654321
Printed in the United States of America

CONTENTS

Dedicated to my son, Michael Green, and to my daughter, Cynthia Green Crider. Thank you for your faith in my ministry and for your walk with God.

ACKNOWLEDGMENTS

I want to give special thanks to all my teachers. We really know nothing we have not learned from a teacher or a prior experience. I am indebted to all who have taught me, both academically and spiritually. Truths gleaned from many sources have become a permanent part of my life, although the sources have long been forgotten. Many of these truths will surface in this book; to all my teachers, I say, "Thank you!"

Finally, a special thank you to Allen Quain, Ginny Maxwell, and the Creation House staff who guided me through the process. For your suggestions and contributions I will always be grateful.

INTRODUCTION

MANY PEOPLE LOOK at a computer and immediately give up on learning to use it. They view it as too complicated and too hard to deal with, having too much to remember. So some interesting, informative, and rather simple books—such as *Computers for Dummies* and *Windows for Dummies*—have been written. By following basic principles in small bites, average people find they can understand more about the world of computers.

The sense of hopelessness in learning to work with computers is also experienced in other areas of life, and this is especially true when many people consider the Bible. They make statements like this: "The Bible is too hard to understand. Only trained professionals, such as ministers, priests, rabbis, and professors of theology can really tell us what it means." This is not true. You can understand the Bible and receive tremendous value from its teaching. You can learn about God. You can find His will for your life. Most importantly, you can learn about God's salvation and receive His eternal life and a heavenly home.

Dr. Robert Schuller, founder of the well-known Crystal Cathedral, made the following statement about big problems, difficult projects, and hopeless situations: "Inch by inch, anything is a cinch." This is an excellent

1

statement, and it offers valuable insight on how to conquer any problem and complete any project, no matter how complicated or hopeless it may seem.

The statement "Ignorance is bliss" is false. Ignorance is a disaster, and the ignorance of God's Word is a great tragedy indeed. God said this about His people, Israel:

> The ox knows its owner and the donkey its master's crib; but Israel does not know, My people do not consider.
>
> —Isaiah 1:3

> My people are destroyed for lack of knowledge. Because you have rejected knowledge, I also will reject you.
>
> —Hosea 4:6

I thought about using the phrase "The Bible for Dummies" as a subtitle for this book. But I think you get the idea. It's easy! No matter how little you know or how confused you may be about the Bible, you will soon have a greater knowledge of the Word of God. The fear that you cannot learn from Scripture will be gone, and you will be on your way to becoming a real Bible student.

This book is offered with the prayer that it might dispel much ignorance about God, His Word, His covenants, His will for our lives, and His plan for humanity.

Chapter 1

ABRAHAM
AND THE COVENANT

W E CANNOT UNDERSTAND God and the way He works until we understand the meaning of covenant relationship. Many covenants are mentioned in the Bible, but the two most important to us are the old covenant and the new covenant.

The word *covenant* is an agreement or contract between two or more persons or parties. When a man and woman marry each other, they enter into a covenant. They promise to love, cherish, respect, and remain faithful to each other as long as they live. If either of them, without cause, leaves the other and begins to live in the same type of relationship with another person, that one has broken the covenant.

In the relationship between workers and the management of a company, the workers are often represented by a labor union. The leaders of the union and the leaders of the company meet together to work out an agreement acceptable to both parties. This agreement is called a contract.

The contract tells what the management expects of the workers and what the workers can expect from the company. It states how much the workers will be paid and explains in great detail the conditions under which they will work. One of the main provisions gives the length of the contract, usually from one to five years.

GOD IS A COVENANT GOD

God is a God of covenant; He made a covenant with a man by the name of Abraham. This covenant not only applied to the relationship between God and Abraham, but it also involved all of Abraham's descendants. It was the beginning of what is known as the old covenant, and the Bible has much to say about this covenant relationship between Abraham and almighty God.

God also made a covenant with mankind through the person of the Lord Jesus Christ, and it is called the new covenant. We will learn much more about the new covenant later. Now, however, we will focus our attention on the old covenant because this is where it all begins.

We have given two examples of earthly, man-made covenants—marriage and labor contracts. However, there is a great deal of difference between a covenant made by two or more human beings and a covenant made by God. In a relationship formed between human parties, both sides have a part in working out the rules and conditions of the contract or agreement. In covenants made by God, it is He who prepares the provisions and makes all the rules.

In God's covenants, He is the superior power. Man must agree to all of God's rules and provisions. Man's covenants are called bilateral covenants; both parties work together equally to reach agreement. God's covenants are unilateral covenants. He is the superior party. God makes the rules; He offers mankind a relationship, and man's only decision is to say yes or no to His offer and His plans. Man cannot change the rules.

The word *covenant* is first used in the Bible in Genesis 6:18, where God made promises to Noah. Later, in Genesis 9, God gave a covenant promise that He would never again send a flood to destroy mankind. God also made covenant with David and others, but all the other covenants flow into or out of the covenant God made with Abraham. When Paul the Apostle says that Jesus fulfilled the covenant, he is speaking of God's covenant with Abraham:

> Now to Abraham and his Seed were the promises made. He does
> not say, "And to seeds," as of many, but as of one, "And to your
> Seed," who is Christ.
>
> —GALATIANS 3:16

When we begin to study this old covenant we immediately meet a man called Abraham. He was first identified as Abram. His family had settled in an area known as Ur of the Chaldeans. It would seem his father, Terah, was an idol worshiper, for it says in Joshua 24:2, "[He] served other gods." Abram left Ur and traveled in the land of Mesopotamia to a place called Haran.

Abram was chosen by God to be the father of a new nation that would be called Israel. We have no idea why he was chosen, only that it was a sovereign act of God. As far as we can tell, Abram seemed to be no different from the others around him. The one thing we know for sure is that he had the ability to hear from God. Israel became the special people of God, the nation from which Jesus the Christ—the great Savior and Deliverer—came. The Bible dramatically tells us how God called Abram:

> Now the Lord had said to Abram: "Get out of your country, From
> your family And from your father's house, To a land that I will
> show you. I will make you a great nation; I will bless you And
> make your name great; And you shall be a blessing. I will bless
> those who bless you, And I will curse him who curses you; And
> in you all the families of the earth shall be blessed."
>
> —GENESIS 12:1–3

SEVEN PROMISES FROM GOD TO ABRAHAM

Although Abram did not realize it, God was beginning to set up the provisions and promises of the covenant He was going to make with him. Here are seven promises recorded in these words from God:

1. I will make you a great nation.
2. I will bless you.
3. And make your name great.
4. And you shall be a blessing.
5. I will bless those who bless you.
6. I will curse him who curses you.

7. And in you, all the families of the earth shall be blessed.

God had directed Abram to leave the country where he was, and Abram, in obedience to God's call, left Haran and traveled to the land of Canaan. It was there God spoke to him again, making additional promises and commitments to him:

> Then the Lord appeared to Abram and said, "To your descendants I will give this land." And there he built an altar to the Lord, who had appeared to him.
>
> —Genesis 12:7

And the Lord said to Abram, after Lot (his nephew) had separated from him:

> Lift your eyes now and look from the place where you are—northward, southward, eastward, and westward; for all the land which you see I give to you and your descendants forever. And I will make your descendants as the dust of the earth; so that if a man could number the dust of the earth, then your descendants also could be numbered. Arise, walk in the land through its length and its width, for I give it to you.
>
> —Genesis 13:14–17

Abram had demonstrated his faith in God's Word and his obedience to God's command, and God was ready to make a covenant between Himself and Abram. As we have said, we call this covenant the old covenant. It is also known as the blood covenant. God gave to Abram the sign of covenant relationship—the shedding of blood, also known as "the cutting of the covenant." It began like this:

> Then He said to him, "I am the Lord, who brought you out of Ur of the Chaldeans, to give you this land to inherit it." And he said, "Lord God, how shall I know that I will inherit it?" So He said to him, "Bring Me a three-year-old heifer, a three-year-old female goat, a three-year-old ram, a turtledove, and a young pigeon." Then he brought all these to Him and cut them in two, down the middle, and placed each piece opposite the other, but he did not cut the birds in two. And when the vultures came down on

the carcasses, Abram drove them away. Now when the sun was going down, a deep sleep fell upon Abram; and behold, horror and great darkness fell upon him. Then He said to Abram: "Know certainly that your descendants will be strangers in a land that is not theirs, and will serve them, and they will afflict them four hundred years. And also the nation whom they serve I will judge; afterward they shall come out with great possessions."

—Genesis 15:7–14

Many important things were happening here. God and Abram were "cutting covenant." They were beginning the most unusual relationship any human ever had with God. As a result, God told Abram some secrets:

1. God promised Abram the land of Canaan, but Abram wanted an assurance.

2. God said to Abram, "You can believe it, because I am going to cut covenant with you." There had been "talk" between Abram and God before, but now their relationship was developing more. God was saying, "My integrity is at stake. I'm confirming my promise to you, and you can count on it."

3. God gave Abram a guarantee, that although his descendants would go through difficult times, they would come forth victorious and return to the land that He had promised them.

On the same day the Lord made a covenant with Abram, saying: "To your descendants I have given this land."

—Genesis 15:18

ABRAHAM'S TRANSFORMATION

This was not the completion of the matter. God was preparing to make a dramatic change in Abram's life, to strengthen His covenant relationship with Abram even more. Notice in the following words how God began to enlarge Abram's understanding of his future and of all the powerful things that were going to happen to him:

When Abram was ninety-nine years old, the Lord appeared to Abram and said to him, "I am Almighty God; walk before Me and be blameless. And I will make My covenant between Me and you, and will multiply you exceedingly." Then Abram fell on his face, and God talked with him, saying: "As for Me, behold, My covenant is with you, and you shall be a father of many nations. No longer shall your name be called Abram [high father], but your name shall be Abraham [father of many nations]; for I have made you a father of many nations. I will make you exceedingly fruitful; and I will make nations of you, and kings shall come from you. And I will establish My covenant between Me and you and your descendants after you in their generations, for an everlasting covenant, to be God to you and your descendants after you."

—GENESIS 17:1–7

After hearing all these exciting things, it was time for Abraham to shed his blood as part of this covenant relationship. God demanded from him the sign of the covenant—circumcision:

And God said to Abraham: "As for you, you shall keep My covenant, you and your descendants after you throughout their generations. This is My covenant which you shall keep, between Me and you and your descendants after you: Every male child among you shall be circumcised; and you shall be circumcised in the flesh of your foreskins, and it shall be a sign of the covenant between Me and you."

—GENESIS 17:9–11

God continued to tell Abraham that every male—the child who was born in his house and all who came to live, work, and identify with him—had to bear this sign of covenant relationship. This was not an elective. It was a command that no one was to refuse:

And the uncircumcised male child, who is not circumcised in the flesh of his foreskin, that person shall be cut off from his people; he has broken My covenant.

—GENESIS 17:14

These were demanding words, but Abraham believed and obeyed God.

> So Abraham took Ishmael his son, all who were born in his house
> and all who were bought with his money, every male among the
> men of Abraham's house, and circumcised the flesh of their fore-
> skins that very same day, as God had said to him.
> —GENESIS 17:23

Abraham had to shed his blood to make the covenant effective. Many others were circumcised in obedience to God's command, but Abraham was the one who cut covenant with God and thus began the covenant relationship.

ISAAC: ABRAHAM'S SACRIFICE

Only twice in the whole Bible does a father offer to sacrifice his only son. Father God offered His Son, Jesus, as a sacrifice at Calvary. Father Abraham offered his son Isaac in sacrifice to God.

When God tested Abraham and asked him to sacrifice his son Isaac, he obeyed. He had great faith, believing God would raise Isaac from the dead. He trusted his covenant God:

> And Abraham stretched out his hand and took the knife to slay
> his son. But the Angel of the Lord called to him from heaven
> and said, "Abraham, Abraham!" So he said, "Here I am." And He
> said, "Do not lay your hand on the lad, or do anything to him; for
> now I know that you fear God, since you have not withheld your
> son, your only son, from Me." Then Abraham lifted his eyes and
> looked, and there behind him was a ram caught in a thicket by its
> horns. So Abraham went and took the ram, and offered it up for a
> burnt offering instead of his son. And Abraham called the name
> of the place, The-Lord-Will-Provide [Jehovah Jireh]; as it is said
> to this day, "In the Mount of the Lord it shall be provided." Then
> the Angel of the Lord called to Abraham a second time out of
> heaven, and said: "By Myself I have sworn, says the Lord, because
> you have done this thing, and have not withheld your son, your
> only son—blessing I will bless you, and multiplying I will multi-
> ply your descendants as the stars of the heaven and as the sand
> which is on the seashore; and your descendants shall possess the

gate of their enemies. In your seed all the nations of the earth shall be blessed, because you have obeyed My voice."

—GENESIS 22:10–18

In the powerful "faith chapter" of Hebrews 11, Abraham's great act of faith is recorded:

By faith Abraham, when he was tested, offered up Isaac, and he who had received the promises offered up his only begotten son, of whom it was said, "In Isaac your seed shall be called," concluding that God was able to raise him up, even from the dead, from which he also received him in a figurative sense.

—HEBREWS 11:17–19

We also know God's covenant blessings continued upon the descendants of Abraham—to his son Isaac, his grandson Jacob, and his great-grandson Joseph. Even when Joseph was sold into slavery by his brothers, "the Lord was with Joseph" (Gen. 39:2, 21), and in God's plan and time he became the "second-in-command" ruler over all Egypt. Joseph's dying words confirmed the covenant God gave to Abraham:

And Joseph said to his brethren, "I am dying; but God will surely visit you, and bring you out of this land to the land of which He swore to Abraham, to Isaac, and to Jacob."

—GENESIS 50:24

As you can see, this covenant was a powerful instrument between God, Abraham, and his descendants, the people of Israel. God gave the provisions of the covenant; but for the covenant to work it would require the faithfulness of God and the obedience of Abraham and his descendants, the nation of Israel. It will be exciting to see how all this works out as we continue our studies.

Chapter 2

God and His Word

WE HAVE TALKED about God and His covenant with Abraham. Now it is time to look at God and see what we can learn about Him. Jesus gave us one of the great revelations about God when He said, "God is Spirit, and those who worship Him must worship in spirit and truth" (John 4:24).

First, when we look at the world around us, the heavens above us, and the earth on which we live, we must start asking ourselves some questions. How did it all get here? Who is the creator of this world and everything in it? There is really only one intelligent answer to these questions: there has to be "a higher power," an intelligent and all-powerful Creator. The Bible identifies this Creator as God.

THE CHRISTIAN AND BIBLE BELIEF

We who are Christians believe there is only one dependable source of information about the world and its Creator. That source is a book called the Bible. At the beginning of the Bible, we start to learn about the One called God. He is the Supreme Being. He has the intelligence and the power to create and maintain all things:

> Therefore know this day, and consider it in your heart, that the Lord Himself is God in heaven above and on the earth beneath; there is no other.
>
> —Deuteronomy 4:39

God is the Source of all life. The wonderful thing about God is that He wants to reveal Himself to us. He wants us to know Him. As Creator, He is our Father, and we are His children:

> God, who made the world and everything in it, since He is Lord of heaven and earth, does not dwell in temples made with hands. Nor is He worshiped with men's hands, as though He needed anything, since He gives to all life, breath, and all things. And He has made from one blood every nation of men to dwell on all the face of the earth, and has determined their preappointed times and the boundaries of their dwellings, so that they should seek the Lord, in the hope that they might grope for Him and find Him, though He is not far from each one of us; for in Him we live and move and have our being, as also some of your own poets have said, "For we are also His offspring."
>
> —Acts 17:24–28

"One blood." This was stated almost two thousand years ago, but it was hundreds of years before scientists discovered the truth of this "one blood" statement. Our blood types are different, but we still cannot differentiate one nation or race from another by blood. But God knew!

Many people have their own ideas about God. Some of these ideas are totally unfounded. But the wonderful thing about God is that we do not have to guess about Him or draw our ideas from the personal philosophies of other people. All we have to do is go to God's book, the Bible, and we can learn some marvelous things about our God. The first and most important thing we learn is that God is the Creator:

> In the beginning God created the heavens and the earth.
>
> —Genesis 1:1

> The heavens declare the glory of God; and the firmament shows His handiwork.
>
> —Psalm 19:1

Four Attributes of God

Four qualities (attributes) describe God. No other person or creature can claim these attributes. Others have attempted to define God, but we turn to the Bible for the final answers and descriptions.

1. God is eternal

> Then Abraham planted a tamarisk tree in Beersheba, and there called on the name of the Lord, the Everlasting God.
>
> —Genesis 21:33

> Lord, You have been our dwelling place in all generations. Before the mountains were brought forth, or ever You had formed the earth and the world, Even from everlasting to everlasting, You are God.
>
> —Psalm 90:1–2

2. God is omnipotent—almighty, all-powerful

> When Abram was ninety-nine years old, the Lord appeared to Abram and said to him, "I am Almighty God; walk before Me and be blameless."
>
> —Genesis 17:1

> But Jesus looked at them [His disciples] and said to them, "With men this is impossible, but with God all things are possible."
>
> —Matthew 19:26

> And I heard, as it were, the voice of a great multitude, as the sound of many waters and as the sound of mighty thunderings, saying, "Alleluia! For the Lord God Omnipotent reigns!"
>
> —Revelation 19:6

3. God is omniscient—all-knowing

> For there is not a word on my tongue, but behold, O Lord, You know it altogether.
>
> —Psalm 139:4

> God is greater than our heart, and knows all things.
>
> —1 John 3:20

And there is no creature hidden from His sight, but all things are naked and open to the eyes of Him to whom we must give account.

—Hebrews 4:13

4. God is omnipresent—present everywhere, unlimited by space

"Can anyone hide himself in secret places, so I shall not see him?" says the Lord; "Do I not fill heaven and earth?" says the Lord.

—Jeremiah 23:24

Where can I go from Your Spirit? Or where can I flee from Your presence? If I ascend into heaven, You are there; if I make my bed in hell, behold, You are there.

—Psalm 139:7–8

Thus says the Lord: "Heaven is My throne, and earth is My footstool."

—Isaiah 66:1

When people in the Bible had contact with God, they wanted to know what to call Him. They wanted to know God's name. In our English Bible, the word *Jehovah* is used as the name for God. The meaning of Jehovah is "I AM" or "the Eternal One." In addition, many compound names are used for God, and each one reveals something of His nature and His character. God is also revealed in the Bible as Father, Son, and Holy Spirit. (See pages 22–23 for a listing of some of these compound names of God.)

In the New Testament, Jesus is revealed as the great "I AM":

And He said to them, "You are from beneath; I am from above. You are of this world; I am not of this world."

—John 8:23

Jesus said to them, "Most assuredly, I say to you, before Abraham was, I AM."

—John 8:58

Jesus is also identified with the Holy Spirit because of the Holy Spirit's activity in His life and ministry. The Holy Spirit reveals the anointing of

God, and Jesus is called "the Christ" or "the Anointed One":

> Therefore let all the house of Israel know assuredly that God has made this Jesus, whom you crucified, both Lord and Christ. [He is the Anointed One, the Messiah.]
>
> —ACTS 2:36

Jesus was the revelation and manifestation of God. We therefore understand that He was "God in the flesh." Jesus was not all of God, but in Him "all the fullness of the Godhead in bodily form was dwelling [revealed]" (Col. 2:9, author's paraphrase):

> In the beginning was the Word, and the Word was with God, and the Word was God...And the Word became flesh and dwelt among us, and we beheld His glory, the glory as of the only begotten of the Father, full of grace and truth.
>
> —JOHN 1:1, 14

THE BIBLE

We have said we learn about God in the Bible. The logical question we should ask is: What is the Bible? And the simplest answer is the best answer. The Bible is the Word of God in written form. The Bible was written by holy men of God. The Holy Spirit moved upon certain prophets and priests to write the thirty-nine books that make up the Old Testament. The same Holy Spirit moved upon apostles and evangelists to write the twenty-seven books of the New Testament.

Therefore, we say that the Bible (the Scriptures) was produced by the inspiration of God through the Holy Spirit. This concept of the inspiration of God means that God the Holy Spirit moved upon men to write; He breathed into their minds the very thoughts they expressed, and He guided them in the words they wrote:

> For prophecy never came by the will of man, but holy men of God spoke as they were moved by the Holy Spirit.
>
> —2 PETER 1:21

> For this reason we also thank God without ceasing, because when you received the word of God which you heard from us,

you welcomed it not as the word of men, but as it is in truth, the word of God, which also effectively works in you who believe.

—1 Thessalonians 2:13

The good news is this: the God who created us and loves us also wants us to know Him and have a relationship with Him now and through all eternity. In order to accomplish this, He has given us this marvelous book we call the Bible.

In the Bible, God's purpose is to train us in a correct and holy lifestyle and give us instructions concerning His salvation—the gift of eternal life.

In human society, the greater does not usually seek a relationship with the lesser. The business world and the military world are good examples. We are grateful that the omnipotent God wants a relationship—fellowship with His creation. He wants to give us direction:

Your word is a lamp to my feet and a light to my path.

—Psalm 119:105

[Paul to Timothy] From childhood you have known the Holy Scriptures, which are able to make you wise for salvation through faith which is in Christ Jesus. All Scripture is given by inspiration of God, and is profitable for doctrine, for reproof, for correction, for instruction in righteousness, that the man of God may be complete, thoroughly equipped for every good work.

—2 Timothy 3:15–17

How We Can Use the Bible

We have some important questions to ask at this time: How do we use the Bible? What can we learn from the Bible? The answers to these and other questions can be summed up in these statements: we should diligently and reverently read and study the Bible. We should believe the Bible is the Word of God, which speaks and communicates to us, and we should use it as our guide for daily living.

The reason we should honor the Bible so highly is that God honors it highly, even magnifying it above His name. "For You have magnified Your word above all Your name" (Ps. 138:2).

Here are some important things we learn from the Bible:

The Scriptures tell us about Jesus.

> You search the Scriptures, for in them you think you have eternal life; and these are they which testify of Me.
>
> —JOHN 5:39

We are blessed when we obey God's Word, the Bible.

In Luke 11:28 Jesus said, "Blessed are those who hear the word of God and keep it!" Jesus was God manifested in human form. We can sum up the identity of Jesus in these words:

- He is called Lord—the Jehovah of the Old Testament.

- He is called Jesus—the earthly name, the name of His humanity.

- He is called the Christ—the name designating the Spirit, the Anointed One, and the Messiah.

We will not sin against God if we live in obedience to the Bible.

> Your word I have hidden in my heart, that I might not sin against You.
>
> —PSALM 119:11

One of the most unusual things about the Bible is that it is not just one book, but a collection of sixty-six books bound together with a tremendous message from God to the human race. The sixty-six books were written by forty-four people over a time period of approximately two thousand years. Through the power and guidance of the Holy Spirit, God used these men to produce a perfect harmony of doctrine and a true declaration of history.

TWO DIVISIONS OF THE BIBLE

There are two major divisions in the Bible—the Old Testament (covenant) and the New Testament (covenant). The Old Testament can be divided into five categories. The New Testament can also be divided into five categories.

OLD TESTAMENT				
The Law (5 books)	**History (12 books)**	**Poetry (5 books)**	**Major Prophets (5 books)**	**Minor Prophets (12 books)**
Genesis	Joshua	Job	Isaiah	Hosea
Exodus	Judges	Psalms	Jeremiah	Joel
Leviticus	Ruth	Proverbs	Lamenta-	Amos
Numbers	1 Samuel	Ecclesiastes	tions	Obadiah
Deuteron-	2 Samuel	Song of	Ezekiel	Jonah
omy	1 Kings	Solomon	Daniel	Micah
	2 Kings			Nahum
	1 Chronicles			Habakkuk
	2 Chronicles			Zephaniah
	Ezra			Haggai
	Nehemiah			Zechariah
	Esther			Malachi

NEW TESTAMENT				
The Gospels (4 books)	**History (1 book)**	**Pauline Epistles (14 books)**	**General Epistles (7 books)**	**Prophecy (1 book)**
Matthew	The Acts of	Romans	James	The Revela-
Mark	the Apostles	1 Corinthians	1 Peter	tion
Luke		2 Corinthians	2 Peter	
John		Galatians	1 John	
		Ephesians	2 John	
		Philippians	3 John	
		Colossians	Jude	
		1 Thessalo-		
		nians		
		2 Thessalo-		
		nians		
		1 Timothy		
		2 Timothy		
		Titus		
		Philemon		
		Hebrews		

When we obey the Bible, we prove our love for Jesus.

> Then Jesus said to those Jews who believed Him, "If you abide in My word, you are My disciples indeed. And you shall know the truth, and the truth shall make you free."
>
> —JOHN 8:31–32

> Jesus answered and said to him, "If anyone loves Me, he will keep My word; and My Father will love him, and We will come to him and make Our home with him."
>
> —JOHN 14:23

THE TWO DOCTRINES IN THE BIBLE: THE LAW AND THE GOSPEL

The Law was given to Moses when he went on Mount Sinai and met God. While on the mount, he received two tables of law, written on stone, containing the Ten Commandments. At that time, he also received many other words of instruction for the nation of Israel. These instructions were to guide them in obedience to the God with whom they had made covenant. In addition, the Law is the basis of all human government. Later, we will learn more about the Law, but we can sum up its importance with these words:

> And these words which I command you today shall be in your heart. You shall teach them diligently to your children, and shall talk of them when you sit in your house, when you walk by the way, when you lie down, and when you rise up.
>
> —DEUTERONOMY 6:6–7

The gospel is the "good news" about Jesus and the salvation He offers to us:

> For God so loved the world that He gave His only begotten Son, that whoever believes in Him should not perish but have everlasting life. For God did not send His Son into the world to condemn the world, but that the world through Him might be saved.
>
> —JOHN 3:16–17

For I am not ashamed of the gospel of Christ, for it is the power of God to salvation for everyone who believes, for the Jew first and also for the Greek [Gentile].

—ROMANS 1:16

In this the love of God was manifested toward us, that God has sent His only begotten Son into the world, that we might live through Him.

—1 JOHN 4:9

PAUL SHOWS US THE CONTRAST BETWEEN
THE LAW AND FAITH IN CHRIST

For as many as are of the works of the law are under the curse; for it is written, "Cursed is everyone who does not continue in all things which are written in the book of the law, to do them." But that no one is justified by the law in the sight of God is evident, for "the just shall live by faith." Yet the law is not of faith, but "the man who does them shall live by them." Christ has redeemed us from the curse of the law, having become a curse for us (for it is written, "Cursed is everyone who hangs on a tree"), that the blessing of Abraham might come upon the Gentiles in Christ Jesus, that we might receive the promise of the Spirit through faith...But before faith came, we were kept under guard by the law, kept for the faith which would afterward be revealed. Therefore the law was our tutor [schoolmaster—teacher] to bring us to Christ, that we might be justified by faith.

—GALATIANS 3:10–14, 23–24

The Law brought a curse upon the people, not because it was bad, but because it required perfection. The very moment an individual broke one part of the Law, the wrath and curse of the whole Law descended upon him or her. The purpose of the Law was to reveal us guilty before God and thereby convince us of our need for Jesus Christ and God's grace.

There is a vast difference between the Law and the gospel. The Law sets up the rules of what we can and cannot do. It reveals our sins and shows us the wrath of God upon sin. The gospel is the story of what God has done through the Lord Jesus Christ to provide for our salvation and eternal life.

God's provision for us is called "grace" or "favor." All of the benefits of the gospel come to us by the grace of God, not by our good works:

> Not by works of righteousness which we have done, but according to His mercy He saved us.
>
> —TITUS 3:5

> For what the law could not do in that it was weak through the flesh, God did by sending His own Son in the likeness of sinful flesh, on account of sin: He condemned sin in the flesh.
>
> —ROMANS 8:3

OUR BIBLE—SUCH A VALUABLE BOOK

One of the great miracles of the Bible is the way in which it can affect our lives and minister to our problems and needs. Here are just two examples:

1. It uncovers sins and mistakes and also shows us the way to receive cleansing, forgiveness, and victory:

> How can a young man cleanse his way? By taking heed according to Your word.
>
> —PSALM 119:9

> Your word I have hidden in my heart, That I might not sin against You.
>
> —PSALM 119:11

> For the word of God is living and powerful, and sharper than any two-edged sword, piercing even to the division of soul and spirit, and of joints and marrow, and is a discerner of the thoughts and intents of the heart.
>
> —HEBREWS 4:12

2. It imparts strength and gives direction for our lives:

> Your word is a lamp to my feet and a light to my path.
>
> —PSALM 119:105

But He answered and said, "It is written, 'Man shall not live by bread alone, but by every word that proceeds from the mouth of God.'"

—MATTHEW 4:4

THE BIBLE USES MANY COMPOUND NAMES TO DESCRIBE GOD

Here are some examples:

JEHOVAH TSIDKENU	"Jehovah, Our Righteousness"	Read Rom. 6:23; 1 Pet. 3:18; Rom. 5:17–19.	"For He made Him who knew no sin to be sin for us, that we might become the righteousness of God in Him" (2 Cor. 5:21).
JEHOVAH M'KADDESH	"Jehovah, Our Righteousness"	Read 1 Cor. 6:9–11; 1 Thess. 4:3–4; 5:23; Rom. 6:17–18; Heb. 13:12.	He not only takes away sin, but also breaks its power.
JEHOVAH SHALOM	"Jehovah, Our Peace"	Read Col. 1:20–22; Heb. 10:19–20.	This name represents wholeness and harmony with God, contentment/satisfaction in life.
JEHOVAH SHAMMAH	"Jehovah Is There/Present"	Read Exod. 23:14.	This name represents wholeness and harmony with God, contentment/satisfaction in life.
JEHOVAH ROPHE	"Jehovah Heals"	Read Isa. 53:5; 1 Pet. 2:24; Rom. 14:17.	He restores, cures, heals—physically, spiritually, and morally.

JEHOVAH JIREH	"God's Provision Shall Be Seen"	Read Gen. 22:8, 14.	"He who did not spare His own Son, but delivered Him up for us all, how shall He not with Him also freely give us all things?" (Rom. 8:32).
JEHOVAH ROHI	"Jehovah, My Shepherd"	Read Ps. 23; John 10:11; Heb. 13:20.	Thank God that Jesus is our Shepherd.
JEHOVAH NISSI	"Jehovah, My Banner"	Read Eph. 1:19–22; Rom. 8:31, 37.	This name represents His cause and His battle and is a sign for deliverance, salvation, and victory. "In that day there shall be a Root of Jesse, Who shall stand as a banner to the people." (Isa. 11:10).

Chapter 3

Angels, Lucifer, and Creation

I T SEEMS THE closer we come to the end of this age, the more we hear about angels, demons, and the devil. Hebrews 1:14 speaks of angels and says, "Are they not all ministering spirits sent forth to minister for those who will inherit salvation?" For us, this is a great thing. God sends angels to help us.

Basically, there are two kinds of angels—good angels and bad angels. Many books have been written on the subject of angels, but the simplest way to learn about them is to let the Bible, the Word of God, speak.

First, angels are great in number:

> [At the time when Jesus was born] And suddenly there was with the angel a multitude of the heavenly host praising God and saying: "Glory to God in the highest, And on earth peace, goodwill toward men!"
>
> —LUKE 2:13–14

Second, angels have great power. We learn in 2 Kings 19:35 that when the Assyrian army attacked God's people, one angel killed 185,000 troops under the command of Sennacherib. On another occasion, the prophet Elisha and his servant were protected from a heathen army by a great host of angels (2 Kings 6:15–17):

> Bless the Lord, you His angels, Who excel in strength, who do His word, Heeding the voice of His word.
>
> —PSALM 103:20

Third, angels love to praise and bless the Lord God.

> Praise Him, all His angels; Praise Him, all His hosts!
>
> —PSALM 148:2

> Let them praise the name of the Lord, For He commanded and they were created.
>
> —PSALM 148:5

> Bless the Lord, all you His hosts, You ministers of His, who do His pleasure.
>
> —PSALM 103:21

Fourth, angels serve God's people, especially children.

> For He shall give His angels charge over you, To keep you in all your ways. In their hands they shall bear you up, Lest you dash your foot against a stone.
>
> —PSALM 91:11–12

> [Jesus is speaking about the little children] Take heed that you do not despise one of these little ones, for I say to you that in heaven their angels always see the face of My Father who is in heaven.
>
> —MATTHEW 18:10

In Acts 12:5–11, we read how an angel set the apostle Peter free from prison. The Bible also has some most important things to say about evil angels and demons.

First, evil angels were created holy. They sinned and rebelled against God, and now they are forever rejected by God. Their destiny is in hell:

25

> For if God did not spare the angels who sinned, but cast them down to hell and delivered them into chains of darkness, to be reserved for judgment.
>
> —2 PETER 2:4

Second, evil angels and demons are cunning, powerful, and numerous. They (and their leader, the devil) are very deceiving. Often people ask: How can I keep from being deceived? The answer: deception is corrected by discernment. This is why it is important to know the Word of God and have a strong prayer life. In this way, we can learn the ways of God and the difference between the voice of God and the lies of the devil:

> For we do not wrestle against flesh and blood, but against principalities, against powers, against the rulers of the darkness of this age, against spiritual hosts of wickedness in the heavenly places.
>
> —EPHESIANS 6:12

> [Jesus was casting out demons] Then He asked him, "What is your name?" And he answered, saying, "My name is Legion; for we are many."
>
> —MARK 5:9

> And no wonder! For Satan himself transforms himself into an angel of light.
>
> —2 CORINTHIANS 11:14

Third, evil angels are the enemies of God and man. They are out to destroy man and the works of God. What we read and learn about the devil's agenda is also the agenda and plan of all evil angels and demons:

> [These are the words of Jesus, speaking to the religious leaders of His day.] You are of your father the devil, and the desires of your father you want to do. He was a murderer from the beginning, and does not stand in the truth, because there is no truth in him. When he speaks a lie, he speaks from his own resources, for he is a liar and the father of it.
>
> —JOHN 8:44

Be sober, be vigilant; because your adversary the devil walks about like a roaring lion, seeking whom he may devour. Resist him, steadfast in the faith, knowing that the same sufferings are experienced by your brotherhood in the world.

—1 PETER 5:8–9

It is important to state that we must not become "angel-conscious" and go around looking for angels (or demons) behind every wall. We must not worship angels. Paul the Apostle gives us a final word:

Let no one cheat you of your reward, taking delight in false humility and worship of angels, intruding into those things which he has not seen, vainly puffed up by his fleshly mind.

—COLOSSIANS 2:18

Remember this important word of warning: no angel has authority to change or overcome the Word of God.

But even if we, or an angel from heaven, preach any other gospel to you than what we have preached to you, let him be accursed.

—GALATIANS 1:8

Our greatest protection against all deception is to have a close relationship with, and be a part of a well-balanced, Bible-believing, Bible-teaching, and Bible-practicing local church.

WHAT ABOUT LUCIFER...SATAN...THE DEVIL?

Lucifer started out as the number one angel. He was a beautiful creature—mightily anointed by God—and had access to the very throne of God. When he spoke, it sounded like a great pipe organ. When he was created by God, he was perfect in beauty and wisdom. Here is how the Bible describes him:

You were the seal of perfection, full of wisdom and perfect in beauty. You were in Eden, the garden of God; every precious stone was your covering: The sardius, topaz, and diamond, beryl, onyx, and jasper, sapphire, turquoise, and emerald with gold. The workmanship of your timbrels and pipes was prepared for you on the day you were created. You were the anointed cherub who covers; I established you; you were on the holy mountain of God; you walked back and forth in the midst of fiery stones.

—EZEKIEL 28:12–14

SO WHAT HAPPENED TO THIS WONDERFUL CREATURE?

Something the Bible calls "iniquity" got into him. This iniquity was basically pride, leading to open rebellion against almighty God. He rose up against God and actually attempted to overthrow the throne of God. He wanted to take God's place, to become God! Instead, he became the devil, and one third of all the angels followed him. God put them out of heaven. Again, we will let the Bible tell the story:

> How you are fallen from heaven, O Lucifer, son of the morning! How you are cut down to the ground, you who weakened the nations! For you have said in your heart: "I will ascend into heaven, I will exalt my throne above the stars of God; I will also sit on the mount of the congregation on the farthest sides of the north; I will ascend above the heights of the clouds, I will be like the Most High." [But here is God's answer:] Yet you shall be brought down to Sheol, to the lowest depths of the Pit.
>
> —ISAIAH 14:12–15

> You were perfect in your ways from the day you were created, till iniquity was found in you.... Your heart was lifted up because of your beauty; You corrupted your wisdom for the sake of your splendor; I cast you to the ground, I laid you before kings, that they might gaze at you.
>
> —EZEKIEL 28:15, 17

It is important that we do not let pride take hold of us. Every good thing we possess—all the power, all the anointing—are from God. When we start exalting ourselves, we are heading for serious trouble. This is especially true with godly leaders!

28

What About the Devil and His Demons Now? Should We Be Afraid?

Lucifer and all the angels who followed him are fallen from heaven. Some are held captive until the judgment day; others roam the earth. They (Lucifer and his angels) are cunning and powerful. They are enemies of God and all the children of God. Here are some Bible facts about Lucifer and his demons.

Second Peter 2:4 tells us, "God did not spare the angels who sinned, but cast them down to hell and delivered them into chains of darkness, to be reserved for judgment." In the little Book of Jude, verse 6 says, "And the angels who did not keep their proper domain, but left their own abode, He has reserved in everlasting chains under darkness for the judgment of the great day."

We should not fear the devil because we have power over him in the name of Jesus. Nevertheless, we must remember this warning by the apostle Peter:

> Be sober, be vigilant; because your adversary the devil walks about like a roaring lion, seeking whom he may devour. Resist him, steadfast in the faith, knowing that the same sufferings are experienced by your brotherhood in the world.
>
> —1 Peter 5:8–9

Satan's Final Home

When it is all over, the devil has a place he must go. It is called "hell." Hell was made not for man, but for the devil and his angels. The only people who will go to hell are those who refuse Jesus, the Lord and Christ. When they reject God, His Son, and His plan, there is no place for them in heaven:

> Then He [King Jesus] will also say to those on the left hand, "Depart from Me, you cursed, into the everlasting fire prepared for the devil and his angels."
>
> —Matthew 25:41

THE FINAL NEWS ON THE SUBJECT OF THE DEVIL IS "GOOD NEWS"

We do not have to fear the devil nor his demons. God, His Son Jesus, and His church all have power over Satan:

> [Jesus said] And these signs will follow those who believe: In My name they will cast out demons.
>
> —MARK 16:17

> Then the seventy returned [to Jesus] with joy, saying, "Lord, even the demons are subject to us in Your name." And He said to them, "I saw Satan fall like lightning from heaven. Behold, I give you the authority to trample on serpents and scorpions, and over all the power of the enemy, and nothing shall by any means hurt you. Nevertheless, do not rejoice in this, that the spirits are subject to you, but rather rejoice because your names are written in heaven."
>
> —LUKE 10:17–20

> [God raised Christ] from the dead and seated Him at His right hand in the heavenly places, far above all principality and power and might and dominion, and every name that is named, not only in this age but also in that which is to come.
>
> —EPHESIANS 1:20–21

Remember, Satan may be powerful, cunning, and deceptive; but the Word of God declares, "He who is in you [in us] is greater than he who is in the world" (1 John 4:4). God's power in us is stronger than the devil's power.

THE CREATION

Before God created the earth, he had already created the angels; but the beginning, as it pertains to us, started with the physical creation of the heavens and the earth (our universe):

> Where were you when I laid the foundations of the earth? Tell Me, if you have understanding....Or who laid its cornerstone

when the morning stars sang together, and all the sons of God shouted for joy?

—Job 38:4, 6–7

In the beginning God created the heavens and the earth.

—Genesis 1:1

By faith we understand that the worlds were framed by the word of God, so that the things which are seen were not made of things which are visible.

—Hebrews 11:3

There is much discussion about our earth and how it was created, but one thing we know for sure: whenever it was created and however it was created, God did it. In fact, God created everything in heaven and earth, visible and invisible. The Bible tells us that Jesus, the Son of God, was involved in all Creation:

He is the image of the invisible God, the firstborn over all creation. For by Him all things were created that are in heaven and that are on earth, visible and invisible, whether thrones or dominions or principalities or powers. All things were created through Him and for Him. And He is before all things, and in Him all things consist.

—Colossians 1:15–17

The Bible reveals and lists God's act of Creation in the following order. It begins with the spoken word of God, which created light and the firmament and separated the waters so that dry land appeared:

Then God said, "Let there be light"; and there was light.

—Genesis 1:3

Then God said, "Let there be a firmament in the midst of the waters, and let it divide the waters from the waters."

—Genesis 1:6

Then God said, "Let the waters under the heavens be gathered together into one place, and let the dry land appear"; and it was so. And God called the dry land Earth, and the gathering together of the waters He called Seas. And God saw that it was good.

—Genesis 1:9–10

Power to Produce

As we read the Bible, we learn an important lesson. God expects everything He creates to produce. God gave the earth power to produce, to "bring forth" (Gen. 1:24):

And the earth brought forth grass, the herb that yields seed according to its kind, and the tree that yields fruit, whose seed is in itself according to its kind. And God saw that it was good.

—Genesis 1:12

Next, God spoke the heavens into existence. Genesis 1:1 states the fact of His Creation. Genesis 1:16 explains the way this happened, "Then God made two great lights: the greater light [the sun] to rule the day, and the lesser light [the moon] to rule the night. He made the stars also." We know these stars to be other suns in the universe, but God is giving us this word in a way we can understand it. God did not create the world just so He could admire it. He created the earth for "creatures" to live on it and enjoy it:

Then God said, "Let the waters abound with an abundance of living creatures, and let birds fly above the earth across the face of the firmament of the heavens."...Then God said, "Let the earth bring forth the living creature according to its kind: cattle and creeping thing and beast of the earth, each according to its kind"; and it was so. And God made the beast of the earth according to its kind, cattle according to its kind, and everything that creeps on the earth according to its kind. And God saw that it was good.

—Genesis 1:20, 24–25

Here, it is important to notice that one "kind" did not evolve into another "kind," but everything was created "according to its kind." We have already stated God's plan that everything He created was to "bring forth." The land (earth) was to produce plants, but there was more. God also formed every beast of the field and every bird of the air from "out of the ground":

> Out of the ground the Lord God formed every beast of the field and every bird of the air, and brought them to Adam to see what he would call them. And whatever Adam called each living creature, that was its name.
>
> —GENESIS 2:19

NOW ... IT IS "PEOPLE TIME"

Let's see what God had created so far. He had made angels, a world, animals, birds, and water creatures—but God was not finished. He wanted someone with whom He could have fellowship. Here is a revelation secret, not a secret revelation. You can only have complete fellowship with someone who is like you, someone who shares the same interests. But where was God going to find someone like this?

There is only one answer. If God wanted a creature like Himself, He was going to have to make it. And He did. The Bible tells us God created man in His own image, likeness, and character. God gave that man dominion over the whole earth. Man did not evolve from lower creatures, but was created by the direct act of God:

> Then God said, "Let Us make man in Our image, according to Our likeness; let them have dominion over the fish of the sea, over the birds of the air, and over the cattle, over all the earth and over every creeping thing that creeps on the earth."
>
> —GENESIS 1:26

> And the Lord God formed man of the dust of the ground, and breathed into his nostrils the breath of life; and man became a living being.
>
> —GENESIS 2:7

WHAT ABOUT THE UNPROVEN THEORY OF EVOLUTION?

Many people have different ideas about creation. Some, who claim to be highly intelligent and greatly educated, have an idea how all of creation—the world, all animals, human beings, and everything else—came into existence. They believe and teach that it was all an accident, sometimes involving an evolutionary and mysterious process with no explanation.

They teach that even the existence of man was a biological, evolutionary accident with no guiding intelligence.

Webster's Dictionary defines evolution this way: "A process of change in a certain direction; a theory that the various types of animals and plants have their origin in other preexisting types and that the distinguishable differences are due to modification in successive generations."

Evolutionists believe that all things have evolved or developed through long ages, from simple things to more complex forms. Even then, they fail to explain the presence of the simple things. Our basis of belief is the Bible, the Word of God, and the unproven theory of evolution contradicts the Bible's account of the Creation.

Many intelligent teachers accept the explanation that evolution is the source of all life. It is taught in schools as fact. It certainly is not a fact; it is not a reasonable theory; it is only an unsupported hypothesis.

In reality, things do not progress from the simple to the complex. One of the absolute physical laws states that without the operation of an outside force, matter tends to move from "order to disorder." We know there is an outside force that holds everything together. Colossians 1:17 gives us this word about the omnipotent Christ: "And He is before all things, and in Him all things consist." The word *consist* means "strengthened, held together."

We believe the Creation described in the Bible happened in six, twenty-four-hour days. Our reason for believing this comes from Genesis 1:5, 8, 13, 23, and 31 where the Bible states: "The evening and the morning were the _____ day."

Chapter 4

THE STORY OF ADAM AND EVE

THE BIBLE TELLS us that "God is love" (1 John 4:8, 16). The amazing thing about this God of love is that He wants someone with whom He can have fellowship, someone upon whom He can bestow His love. A revelation secret was presented in chapter 3: you can only have complete fellowship with someone who is like you, someone who shares the same interests.

God wanted a creature like Himself, so He created a man; and from this man He created a companion for him. She was called "woman." The Bible gives us the story of this first man and woman, Adam and Eve:

> Then God said, "Let Us make man in Our image, according to Our likeness; let them have dominion over the fish of the sea, over the birds of the air, and over the cattle, over all the earth and over every creeping thing that creeps on the earth." So God created man in His own image; in the image of God He created him; male and female He created them.
>
> —GENESIS 1:26–27

And the Lord God formed man of the dust of the ground, and breathed into his nostrils the breath of life; and man became a living being.

—Genesis 2:7

And the Lord God said, "It is not good that man should be alone; I will make him a helper comparable to him."

—Genesis 2:18

And the Lord God caused a deep sleep to fall on Adam, and he slept; and He took one of his ribs, and closed up the flesh in its place. Then the rib which the Lord God had taken from man He made into a woman, and He brought her to the man. And Adam said: "This is now bone of my bones and flesh of my flesh; she shall be called Woman, because she was taken out of Man. Therefore a man shall leave his father and mother and be joined to his wife, and they shall become one flesh." And they were both naked, the man and his wife, and were not ashamed.

—Genesis 2:21–25

A Man and a Woman With a Mission

When we read that this man and woman were created in the image and likeness of God, it means they were to display His character. God had great plans for Adam and Eve, and He gave them a fourfold mission:

1. They were to fellowship with God and give Him pleasure. The Book of Revelation gives us a great picture of the heavenly scene that confirms this statement:

The twenty-four elders fall down before Him who sits on the throne and worship Him who lives forever and ever, and cast their crowns before the throne, saying: "You are worthy, O Lord, to receive glory and honor and power; for You created all things, and by Your will [desire, pleasure] they exist and were created."

—Revelation 4:10–11

Read Psalm 22:3. Do you feel that our praise brings pleasure to God? Do you feel that joyful praise could bring us into a greater fellowship with God?

> 2. They were to have dominion (rule, power, and authority) over everything God had made:

Then God said, "Let Us make man in Our image, according to Our likeness; let them have dominion over the fish of the sea, over the birds of the air, and over the cattle, over all the earth and over every creeping thing that creeps on the earth."

—GENESIS 1:26

> 3. They were to have children and populate the earth. They were not only to have a special relationship with God, but also to have a special relationship—a special love—with each other. As a result of this love, they, like God, were to have the power of creation. Like everything else God had made, they were to "bring forth":

Then God blessed them, and God said to them, "Be fruitful and multiply; fill the earth and subdue it; have dominion over the fish of the sea, over the birds of the air, and over every living thing that moves on the earth."

—GENESIS 1:28

And Adam called his wife's name Eve, because she was the mother of all living.

—GENESIS 3:20

Now Adam knew [had an intimate, private relationship with] Eve his wife, and she conceived and bore Cain, and said, "I have acquired a man from the Lord."

—GENESIS 4:1

> 4. They were to be the custodians of the garden God planted in Eden:

> The Lord God planted a garden eastward in Eden, and there He
> put the man whom He had formed.
>
> —GENESIS 2:8

SIN ENTERS INTO THE WORLD

In this beautiful garden of God, there were many trees and plants which provided food for Adam and Eve. But there were also two very special trees:

> And out of the ground the Lord God made every tree grow that
> is pleasant to the sight and good for food. The tree of life was also
> in the midst [center] of the garden, and the tree of the knowledge
> of good and evil.
>
> —GENESIS 2:9

God warned Adam and Eve that they were not to eat of the tree of the knowledge of good and evil:

> And the Lord God commanded the man, saying, "Of every tree
> of the garden you may freely eat; but of the tree of the knowledge
> of good and evil you shall not eat, for in the day that you eat of it
> you shall surely die."
>
> —GENESIS 2:16–17

This was not a foolish or vain request. Man was God's creation. He only lived because God gave him life, and all of his wisdom had come from Him. God wanted man to continue to have His government in his life, to depend on Him for his wisdom and power (dominion). The apostle Paul made this clear in Acts 17:28: "For in Him we live and move and have our being [our very existence]...for we are also His offspring."

We do not know when, but we do know that sometime after the Creation of Adam and Eve, the devil—Lucifer—entered the picture. This is the Lucifer who had already committed high treason and rebellion against God, leading one-third of the angelic creation astray. He came to Eve, the woman, in the form of the serpent.

The devil wanted three things to happen:

- He wanted Eve to doubt the Word of God. Isn't this the beginning of unbelief?

- He wanted Eve to desire things forbidden by God. Isn't this where lust begins?

- He wanted Eve to disobey God's command. Isn't this the beginning of rebellion against God?

Now the serpent was more cunning than any beast of the field which the Lord God had made. And he said to the woman, "Has God indeed said, [questioning God, producing doubt] 'You shall not eat of every tree of the garden'?"

And the woman said to the serpent, "We may eat the fruit of the trees of the garden; but of the fruit of the tree which is in the midst of the garden, God has said, 'You shall not eat it, nor shall you touch it, lest you die.'"

Then the serpent said to the woman, "You will not surely die [here he is challenging God's Word]. For God knows that in the day you eat of it your eyes will be opened, and you will be like God, knowing good and evil."

—Genesis 3:1–5

The devil brought three definite areas of temptation to Eve. Here is the Bible's explanation:

So when the woman saw that the tree was good for food [the lust of the flesh], that it was pleasant to the eyes [the lust of the eyes], and a tree desirable to make one wise [the pride of life], she took of its fruit and ate. She also gave to her husband with her, and he ate.

—Genesis 3:6

The New Testament also gives a clear warning about these things:

For all that is in the world—the lust of the flesh, the lust of the eyes, and the pride of life—is not of the Father but is of the world.

—1 John 2:16

As the result of Adam's transgression and disobedience against God's Word, sin infected the entire human race, and death came as a result of the sin:

> Therefore, just as through one man sin entered the world, and death through sin, and thus death spread to all men, because all sinned—For until the law sin was in the world, but sin is not imputed when there is no law. Nevertheless death reigned from Adam to Moses, even over those who had not sinned according to the likeness of the transgression of Adam, who is a type of Him who was to come.
>
> —ROMANS 5:12–14

Before we leave this area of study, turn to Matthew 4:3–11, and read about the devil's temptation of Jesus. See if you can find the same three methods of testing the devil used on Eve.

WE REFER TO ADAM'S SIN AS "THE FALL." WHAT WAS THE RESULT?

The first thing that happened is that Adam and Eve fell from the image and likeness of God. The result was most dramatic:

> Then the eyes of both of them were opened, and they knew that they were naked; and they sewed fig leaves together and made themselves coverings. And they heard the sound of the Lord God walking in the garden in the cool of the day, and Adam and his wife hid themselves from the presence of the Lord God among the trees of the garden.
>
> —GENESIS 3:7–8

Adam's sin was the same as Lucifer's—the sin of rebellion. The Bible says the woman was deceived. Adam was not deceived. He clearly wanted to take the government of his life into his own hands, independent of God. Because of Satan's actions and man's sin, God's sharp words of judgment were spoken to all the characters in this drama.

The serpent was cursed, so the Lord God said to the serpent:

> Because you have done this, you are cursed more than all cattle, and more than every beast of the field; on your belly you shall go, and you shall eat dust all the days of your life. And I will put enmity between you and the woman, and between your seed

and her seed; He shall bruise your head, and you shall bruise His heel.

—GENESIS 3:14–15

We see in these words the promise of the coming Redeemer, Jesus the Christ. He would be "bruised" at the cross, but Satan's head (his power, authority) would be crushed.

God's words to the woman:

> To the woman He said: "I will greatly multiply your sorrow and your conception; in pain you shall bring forth children; your desire shall be for your husband, and he shall rule over you."

—GENESIS 3:16

God's words to the man:

> Then to Adam He said, "Because you have heeded the voice of your wife, and have eaten from the tree of which I commanded you, saying, 'You shall not eat of it': Cursed is the ground for your sake; in toil you shall eat of it all the days of your life. Both thorns and thistles it shall bring forth for you, and you shall eat the herb of the field. In the sweat of your face you shall eat bread till you return to the ground, for out of it you were taken; for dust you are, and to dust you shall return."

—GENESIS 3:17–19

ADAM AND EVE LEAVE THE GARDEN

Some have asked why it was necessary for God to put the man and the woman out of the garden. The answer is simple. They could not be permitted, in their sinful condition, to live in the garden and eat the fruit of the tree of life forever:

> Then the Lord God said, "Behold, the man has become like one of Us, to know good and evil. And now, lest he put out his hand and take also of the tree of life, and eat, and live forever"—therefore the Lord God sent him out of the garden of Eden to till the ground from which he was taken. So He drove out the man; and He placed cherubim [angelic creatures] at the east of the garden

of Eden, and a flaming sword which turned every way, to guard the way to the tree of life.

—GENESIS 3:22–24

On the cross, Jesus suffered and paid the penalty for our sins. Because of His sacrifice, we now have salvation and eternal life. We read in the Book of Revelation about the tree of life being restored:

He who has an ear, let him hear what the Spirit says to the churches. To him who overcomes I will give to eat from the tree of life, which is in the midst of the Paradise of God.

—REVELATION 2:7 (SEE ALSO REVELATION 22:2, 14)

Chapter 5

NOAH

IN THIS CHAPTER, we are going to study about something that had never happened before and will never happen again—the great flood. We have just left the story of Adam and Eve, and we have learned some important lessons as a result of their failure. We can sum up the problem in the garden with these statements: man wanted to be free from God, so he acted in rebellion toward Him. He believed his way was better than God's way. And finally, he had more faith in the words of the serpent (the devil) than in the Word of God.

From the moment Adam sinned, the human race started on a downward spiral. Adam and Eve's first cooperative effort produced a son by the name of Cain. His brother Abel was born later. In a rage of resentment against God and jealousy toward Abel, Cain killed his brother. In one generation, the human race went from Adam's sin of rebellion to the sin of murder.

It did not stop there. God's beautiful creation rapidly became man's sinful society. Human hearts became depraved and corrupt, until you could almost hear God crying out, "That's enough!" You can feel His heart in these words:

Then the Lord saw that the wickedness of man was great in the earth, and that every intent of the thoughts of his heart was only evil continually. And the Lord was sorry that He had made man on the earth, and He was grieved in His heart. So the Lord said, "I will destroy man whom I have created from the face of the earth, both man and beast, creeping thing and birds of the air, for I am sorry that I have made them."

—GENESIS 6:5–7

Into this worldwide corrupted behavior comes one of our great Bible heroes. His name is Noah and, at this time, he becomes the only ray of hope for a sinful, rebellious world:

But Noah found grace in the eyes of the Lord.

—GENESIS 6:8

Immediately we have a question: Who is this fellow Noah? We really do not know. Absolutely nothing is known about his childhood and early life. When he comes on the scene, he is already five hundred years old! We do know a little about his background.

Noah's great-grandfather was a most unusual man by the name of Enoch. When Enoch was sixty-five years old, he had a son by the name of Methuselah (who lived to the age of 969 and became the oldest person who has ever lived). After Methuselah was born, Enoch lived another three hundred years. He walked so closely with God, that when he was 365 years old, God translated him. He did not see death!

Methuselah had a son named Lamech, and Lamech became the father of Noah. "And Noah was five hundred years old, and Noah begot Shem, Ham, and Japheth" (Gen. 5:32). The Bible gives this insight into the character of Noah. "Noah was a just man, perfect in his generations. Noah walked with God" (Gen. 6:9).

THE COMING OF THE FLOOD

God was getting ready to use this man Noah, the one who had "found grace" in His eyes, the man who was "just [righteous]" and "perfect," the one who "walked with God" (Gen. 6:8–9). He was an outstanding man, and God revealed to him that a great flood would cover the earth, destroying all mankind. God gave this man Noah a massive assignment:

> Make yourself an ark of gopherwood [cypress]; make rooms in
> the ark, and cover it inside and outside with pitch. And this is
> how you shall make it: The length of the ark shall be three hun-
> dred cubits, its width fifty cubits, and its height thirty cubits. You
> shall make a window for the ark, and you shall finish it to a cubit
> from above; and set the door of the ark in its side. You shall make
> it with lower, second, and third decks.
> —GENESIS 6:14–16

We do not know the exact size of this boat, because there are differ-
ing beliefs about the size of a cubit. The best estimate is that the ark was
over five hundred feet long, almost one hundred feet wide and over fifty
feet high.

The important thing to remember about Noah is that he believed God.
He was faithful, and he was obedient. Genesis 6:22 says that he did "all
that God commanded him." In return, God trusted Noah and told him
about His plans:

> And behold, I Myself am bringing floodwaters on the earth, to
> destroy from under heaven all flesh in which is the breath of
> life; everything that is on the earth shall die. But I will establish
> My covenant with you; and you shall go into the ark—you, your
> sons, your wife, and your sons' wives with you [a total of eight
> people].
> —GENESIS 6:17–18

Noah brought animals into the ark, two by two, male and female of
each kind. He brought in seven pairs of birds. When everyone was in the
ark, God closed the only door. A great rain fell, and everyone outside the
ark—every living thing, man, and beast—was destroyed. Before the flood,
Noah must have been a laughingstock to the ungodly world around him.
The Bible calls him a "preacher of righteousness" in 2 Peter 2:5. The story
is summed up in the New Testament with these words:

> By faith Noah, being divinely warned of things not yet seen,
> moved with godly fear, prepared an ark for the saving of his

household, by which he condemned the world and became heir
of the righteousness which is according to faith.

—HEBREWS 11:7

When the floodwaters went down, Noah and his family stepped out on
a different earth. "Then Noah built an altar to the Lord, and took of every
clean animal and of every clean bird, and offered burnt offerings on the
altar" (Gen. 8:20). This is the first time the word *altar* is used in the Bible.

GOD'S COVENANT PROMISES TO NOAH

As a result of Noah's obedience, God gave instructions and made some
promises to him:

- God told him and his family to be fruitful and multiply and
  replenish the earth.

- God put the fear of man on all animal and fish life, and the
  earth's creatures were given to man for food.

- God promised He would not curse the ground anymore for
  man's sake.

- God promised He would never again destroy every living
  thing.

- God promised that the seasons and seedtime and harvest
  would continue on the earth.

So God blessed Noah and his sons, and said to them: "Be fruitful
and multiply, and fill the earth. And the fear of you and the dread
of you shall be on every beast of the earth, on every bird of the air,
on all that move on the earth, and on all the fish of the sea. They
are given into your hand. Every moving thing that lives shall be
food for you. I have given you all things, even as the green herbs."

—GENESIS 9:1–3

And the Lord smelled a soothing aroma. Then the Lord said in
His heart, "I will never again curse the ground for man's sake,

although the imagination of man's heart is evil from his youth; nor will I again destroy every living thing as I have done. While the earth remains, seedtime and harvest, cold and heat, winter and summer, and day and night shall not cease."

—GENESIS 8:21–22

THE SIGN OF THE RAINBOW

God also promised Noah that He would never again use a flood to destroy the people of the earth. To confirm this covenant promise, God gave a sign:

I set My rainbow in the cloud, and it shall be for the sign of the covenant between Me and the earth…and I will remember My covenant which is between Me and you and every living creature of all flesh; the waters shall never again become a flood to destroy all flesh. The rainbow shall be in the cloud, and I will look on it to remember the everlasting covenant between God and every living creature of all flesh that is on the earth.

—GENESIS 9:13, 15–16

We wish we could say everything went well on the earth after the flood, but we cannot! Sin was still in the world, and the Redeemer (Jesus) had not yet come. Nimrod, a descendant of Noah's son Ham, became a mighty hunter. And it was this Nimrod who built a kingdom called Babel, the beginning of the Babylonian civilization. The word Babylon means "confusion." When man tries to build anything without God, confusion is always the result.

Man was still a rebel against God. He still felt he could take care of himself and walk his way in life. Remember, this was Adam's problem. Now men began to build a human civilization with the intent of succeeding without God's wisdom and leadership. In the land of Shinar (Babylonia), they built a city and a great tower to accomplish this purpose:

Now the whole earth had one language and one speech. And it came to pass, as they journeyed from the east, that they found a plain in the land of Shinar, and they dwelt there. Then they said to one another, "Come, let us make bricks and bake them thoroughly." They had brick for stone, and they had asphalt for mortar.

> And they said, "Come, let us build ourselves a city, and a tower whose top is in the heavens; let us make a name for ourselves, lest we be scattered abroad over the face of the whole earth."
>
> —GENESIS 11:1–4

This act demonstrated mankind's desire to act independently of God. They wanted to build a great empire that would glorify man and not God. They also proved they did not trust God. He had promised never to destroy the earth by water, but they decided to build the tower—just in case! They were also satanic in their attitude about the tower. Just as Satan had desired to ascend to the throne of God, so man was reaching for the heavens by his own power and might. They said, "Come, let us build ourselves a city, and a tower whose top is in the heavens; let us make a name for ourselves, lest we be scattered abroad over the face of the whole earth" (Gen. 11:4).

WHY DID GOD STOP THE BUILDING
OF THE TOWER?

God moved to stop the building of the tower. Why? Was God afraid? Of course not! He is God almighty and has no reason to fear. But God wanted to demonstrate His wrath against their rebellion. God hates the independent spirit of man that says, "I can make it without God." God did not want a concentration of evil around this monument, so He did a strange thing. He confused the tongues (languages, speech) of the people:

> But the Lord came down to see the city and the tower which the sons of men had built. And the Lord said, "Indeed the people are one and they all have one language, and this is what they begin to do; now nothing that they propose to do will be withheld from them. Come, let Us go down and there confuse their language, that they may not understand one another's speech." So the Lord scattered them abroad from there over the face of all the earth, and they ceased building the city. Therefore its name is called Babel, because there the Lord confused the language of all the earth; and from there the Lord scattered them abroad over the face of all the earth.
>
> —GENESIS 11:5–9

The word *Babylon* has different meanings to different people. To man, and in the language of the Babylonians, it meant "the gate of God." They felt their tower, their city, and all their labors were the way to God. However, God called it "confusion," literally "a confusing sound of voices without coherence or meaning."

What is the important lesson for us? We must not let others draw us into a "Babylonian enterprise." Many clubs, associations, groups, and even religious entities are being formed these days. We must not be too quick to join everything that comes down the road.

At the end of the age, God will deal with every Babylonian system in a most harsh way. As we close this chapter, we leave you with God's final Word:

> After these things I saw another angel coming down from heaven, having great authority, and the earth was illuminated with his glory. And he cried mightily with a loud voice, saying, "Babylon the great is fallen, is fallen, and has become a dwelling place of demons, a prison for every foul spirit, and a cage for every unclean and hated bird!" ... And I heard another voice from heaven saying, "Come out of her, my people, lest you share in her sins, and lest you receive of her plagues."
>
> —REVELATION 18:1–2, 4

> Christ also loved the church and gave Himself for her.
>
> —EPHESIANS 5:25

What a contrast between man's Babylon and the Lord's church!

General references to Noah:

- Genesis, chapters 5–9
- Matthew 24:37
- Hebrews 11:7
- 1 Peter 3:20
- 2 Peter 2:5

Chapter 6

ISRAEL:
THE COVENANT PEOPLE

WE HAVE STUDIED about Abraham and his call from God. One of the promises God gave to Abraham was this: "I will make you a great nation" (Gen. 12:2). This nation became known as Israel. The way this nation received its name is an amazing story. Abraham's grandson Jacob had used trickery to take the place of his older brother, Esau, when it was time to receive their father's blessing and the birthright that was to come to the oldest son.

It is easy to understand that Esau was not pleased with Jacob's conduct. Fearing for his life, Jacob ran away and stayed at his uncle's house for many years. During this time, he married his wives Leah and Rachael and had many children. One day it was time for Jacob to go home, but he still feared his brother. On his way home, he had a life-changing experience. He met God in a place called Peniel. The Bible tells the story:

> Then Jacob was left alone; and a Man wrestled with him until the breaking of day. Now when He saw that He did not prevail against him, He touched the socket of his hip; and the socket of

Jacob's hip was out of joint as He wrestled with him. And He said, "Let Me go, for the day breaks." But he said, "I will not let You go unless You bless me!" So He said to him, "What is your name?" He said, "Jacob." And He said, "Your name shall no longer be called Jacob, but Israel; for you have struggled with God and with men, and have prevailed."

—Genesis 32:24–28

The people of Israel began with the sons of Jacob, after his name was changed to Israel. Joseph, one of Jacob's (Israel's) sons, was sold into slavery by his brothers and was taken to Egypt. Through the divine intervention of God, Joseph became the second ruler in Egypt.

During the time of great famine, he brought his entire family to Egypt. There, over a period of four hundred years, these "children of Israel" grew into a mighty nation—the nation of Israel. The Bible gives a full account of this story in Genesis, chapters 37–50.

Years passed, and Joseph's influence in Egypt had long faded. Great persecution arose, and the Israelites became slaves in Egypt. Finally, the decree went out that all the boy babies of Israel were to be killed at birth. The people cried to God for help, and the Bible says, "God heard their groaning, and God remembered His covenant with Abraham, with Isaac, and with Jacob" (Exod. 2:24). After four hundred years, it was time for Israel to leave Egypt. God's prophetic word to Abraham gives us understanding. In Genesis 15:13–14, God had told Abraham his descendants would be afflicted, but they would come out of Egypt victorious, with great wealth. God promised severe judgment upon Egypt.

Moses, the Deliverer

When the command came to kill all the boy babies of Israel, one couple refused. They hid their baby in a small ark and set it drifting in the river. He was discovered by Pharaoh's daughter, who had him pulled out of the water. She named him Moses, which means "drawn out." He was reared, educated, and trained in Pharaoh's palace:

But when the time of the promise drew near which God had sworn to Abraham, the people grew and multiplied in Egypt till another king arose who did not know Joseph. This man dealt treacherously with our people, and oppressed our forefathers, making them expose their babies, so that they might not live. At this time Moses was born, and was well pleasing to God; and he was brought up in his father's house for three months. But when he was set out, Pharaoh's daughter took him away and brought him up as her own son. And Moses was learned in all the wisdom of the Egyptians, and was mighty in words and deeds.

—Acts 7:17–22

When Moses was forty years old, he attempted to fight for the people of Israel, killing an Egyptian who was persecuting them. Strangely enough, the people rejected him, and he ran away to the land of Midian. There he married and had at least two sons (Exod. 4:20). But God was not finished with Moses. While he was keeping the flock of Jethro, his father-in-law, he had a life-changing experience with God. The story is told in beautiful fashion by Stephen, a deacon in the church at Jerusalem:

And when forty years had passed [Moses was now eighty years old.], an Angel of the Lord appeared to him in a flame of fire in a bush, in the wilderness of Mount Sinai. When Moses saw it, he marveled at the sight; and as he drew near to observe, the voice of the Lord came to him, saying, "I am the God of your fathers—the God of Abraham, the God of Isaac, and the God of Jacob." And Moses trembled and dared not look. Then the Lord said to him, "Take your sandals off your feet, for the place where you stand is holy ground. I have surely seen the oppression of My people who are in Egypt; I have heard their groaning and have come down to deliver them. And now come, I will send you to Egypt." This Moses whom they rejected, saying, "Who made you a ruler and a judge?" is the one God sent to be a ruler and a deliverer by the hand of the Angel who appeared to him in the bush. He brought them out, after he had shown wonders and signs in the land of Egypt, and in the Red Sea, and in the wilderness forty years.

—Acts 7:30–36

After this encounter with God, Moses (with his brother, Aaron) was sent back to Egypt with a message from God for Pharaoh: "Let My people go!" Pharaoh refused and hardened his heart in rebellion. God sent ten different, awful plagues upon Egypt. The last plague upon the nation that had killed Israel's babies was the death of the firstborn child in every Egyptian family.

By this time, Pharaoh had enough and told Moses to take the people and leave Egypt. As they traveled toward the Red Sea, Pharaoh changed his mind again and the armies of Egypt came behind Israel to destroy them. Moses said to the people, "Do not be afraid. Stand still, and see the salvation [deliverance] of the Lord." He told them, "This will be the last time you will see these Egyptians. The Lord will fight for you" (Exod. 14:13–14, author's paraphrase).

The Lord divided the waters, and the people of Israel went through the sea, walking on dry ground. When Pharaoh's army tried to follow them, the waters came together again, and the Egyptians were destroyed. With their enemy gone, they were now free. But what would they do? How would they survive? How would they be governed? We are about to find the answers to these questions—and many more.

ISRAEL AND THE LAW OF GOD

After they left Egypt, Israel was ruled by a theocracy, the rule of God. Moses took the people back to the place where he had seen the burning bush, to a mountain called Sinai. Here God confirmed the special relationship He had with Israel. No nation in history ever received such a marvelous word from God as the statement we are about to read:

> And Moses went up to God, and the Lord called to him from the mountain, saying, "Thus you shall say to the house of Jacob, and tell the children of Israel: 'You have seen what I did to the Egyptians, and how I bore you on eagles' wings and brought you to Myself. Now therefore, if you will indeed obey My voice and keep My covenant, then you shall be a special treasure to Me above all people; for all the earth is Mine. And you shall be to Me a kingdom of priests and a holy nation.' These are the words which you shall speak to the children of Israel."
>
> —EXODUS 19:3–6

It was on this mountain God gave Moses the Law to govern Israel. The Ten Commandments are often called "the Law," but they are only a part of the Law. Many have asked: What was the purpose of the Law? The answer is in three parts.

THE PURPOSE OF THE LAW

1. To teach the people the knowledge of sin. Paul the Apostle confirms this:

Therefore by the deeds of the law no flesh will be justified in His sight, for by the law is the knowledge of sin.

—ROMANS 3:20

What shall we say then? Is the law sin? Certainly not! On the contrary, I would not have known sin except through the law. For I would not have known covetousness unless the law had said, "You shall not covet."

—ROMANS 7:7

2. The Law was a schoolmaster (child trainer) to lead Israel to Christ:

What purpose then does the law serve? It was added because of transgressions, till the Seed should come to whom the promise was made…Therefore the law was our tutor [schoolmaster] to bring us to Christ, that we might be justified by faith.

—GALATIANS 3:19, 24

3. God viewed Israel as His special treasure, and He gave His people the Law to keep them in obedience to their covenant relationship and responsibilities:

Now therefore, if you will indeed obey My voice and keep My covenant, then you shall be a special treasure to Me above all people; for all the earth is Mine.

—EXODUS 19:5

In the beginning, at the time of creation, God wrote His moral law in the very heart of man. This kind of relationship was lost when Adam rebelled in the garden. Because of Adam's transgression, sin entered the world, and now the rules were changed. God called Moses to the top of Mount Sinai, and there He gave him the Law. The Ten Commandments contain the basic summary of the whole Law. We could spend a whole chapter on every commandment, but we will briefly state and explain each of them at this time. You can read them in Exodus 20:3–17.

The first commandment: "You shall have no other gods before Me."

This teaches that there is only one true God, who alone is worthy of our love and worship. If anyone has, serves, worships, or adores any other god (persons, places, or things), that one is guilty of idolatry. Jesus had strong words on this subject. When Satan tempted Him to perform "devil worship," Jesus said, "Away with you, Satan! For it is written, 'You shall worship the Lord your God, and Him only you shall serve'" (Matt. 4:10).

The second commandment: "You shall not make for yourself a carved [graven] image."

God specifically condemned the worship (adoration) of any image (persons, places, or things). God is Spirit, and we must not make any idol of a god or religious figure. Exodus 32 tells how Israel worshiped a golden calf while Moses was receiving the Law on Mount Sinai. Many were destroyed for this great sin:

> I am the Lord, that is My name; and My glory I will not give to another, nor My praise to carved images.
> —ISAIAH 42:8

Today we would include pictures as an image forbidden in this command.

The third commandment: "You shall not take the name of the LORD your God in vain."

We must not use God's name lightly, in a foolish manner or in cursing (swearing). We may call upon His name in prayer, in the hour of need; but we must never do it in a deceitful or hypocritical manner, "For the Lord will not hold him guiltless who takes His name in vain" (Exod. 20:7).

The fourth commandment: "Remember the Sabbath day, to keep it holy."

Here, we learn the principle of God's rest. In the New Testament, the

Sabbath as a "day" (and all other "holy days") was abolished by God Himself. Now, the Lord Jesus Christ is our sabbath rest. Christians are not commanded to observe any day above the other. The early Christian church met on the first day of the week. They called this "the Lord's day":

> [To the hypocritical religious leaders, Jesus said,] The Sabbath was made for man, and not man for the Sabbath. Therefore the Son of Man is also Lord of the Sabbath.
>
> —MARK 2:27–28

> Now on the first day of the week, when the disciples came together to break bread, Paul, ready to depart the next day, spoke to them and continued his message until midnight.
>
> —ACTS 20:7

> On the first day of the week let each one of you lay something aside [bring your offerings].
>
> —1 CORINTHIANS 16:2

> So let no one judge you in food or in drink, or regarding a festival or a new moon or sabbaths, which are a shadow of things to come, but the substance is of Christ.
>
> —COLOSSIANS 2:16–17

The fifth commandment: "Honor your father and your mother, that your days may be long upon the land which the LORD your God is giving you."

The Bible teaches us to not only honor our natural parents, but to give honor to our spiritual leaders. Paul considered these words very important:

> Children, obey your parents in the Lord, for this is right. "Honor your father and mother," which is the first commandment with promise: "that it may be well with you and you may live long on the earth."
>
> —EPHESIANS 6:1–3

> Do not rebuke an older man, but exhort him as a father, younger men as brothers... Let the elders who rule well be counted worthy of double honor, especially those who labor in the word and

doctrine…Do not receive an accusation against an elder except from two or three witnesses.

—1 TIMOTHY 5:1, 17, 19

The sixth commandment: "You shall not murder."

God does not give us as individual human beings the authority to kill others. Our lives are very valuable. If we take the life of another person, or even our own life, this is wrong. In the New Testament (covenant) we must not hate our brother or sister, for "Whoever hates his brother is a murderer" (1 John 3:15). The Bible does give government (the people) the power to punish evildoers:

> Whoever sheds man's blood, by man his blood shall be shed; for in the image of God He made man.
>
> —GENESIS 9:6

The seventh commandment: "You shall not commit adultery."

Sexual relations outside of marriage are sinful. Marriage is intended to be a lifelong union between one man and one woman. Jesus said this about sexual sins: "Whoever looks at a woman [or man] to lust for her has already committed adultery with her in his heart" (Matt. 5:28). Here we are dealing not just with the act but with the heart. This is more than a moment of temptation. It is forming the act in your mind, creating a fantasy. Temptation comes to every human being, but the Bible tells us how to deal with it:

> Flee [run away from] also youthful lusts; but pursue [run toward] righteousness, faith, love, peace with those who call on the Lord out of a pure heart.
>
> —2 TIMOTHY 2:22

It is hard to think about sinful, lustful things while you are calling on the name of the Lord with a pure heart.

The eighth commandment: "You shall not steal."

This is taking something that does not belong to you; but it is also more than that. This commandment deals with every kind of theft and fraud. If we owe a debt and do not pay it, we are stealing. It is wrong if we do not pay those who have worked for us:

> Woe to him who builds his house by unrighteousness and his chambers by injustice, who uses his neighbor's service without wages and gives him nothing for his work.
>
> —Jeremiah 22:13

The ninth commandment: "You shall not bear false witness against your neighbor."

The clear teaching here is that we must avoid all lies, slander, and false statements of any kind against our neighbors, friends, and everyone around us. In fact, we must speak the truth with love and defend our neighbors. If we cannot speak well of them, we should say nothing:

> A talebearer reveals secrets, but he who is of a faithful spirit conceals a matter.
>
> —Proverbs 11:13

> Moreover if your brother sins against you, go and tell him his fault between you and him alone. If he hears you, you have gained your brother.
>
> —Matthew 18:15

> Therefore, putting away lying, "Let each one of you speak truth with his neighbor," for we are members of one another.
>
> —Ephesians 4:25

Sometimes we could tell the truth about another person, but it would be better left unsaid. There are three ways to test the difference between gossip and encouragement: First, is it true? Second, will it edify (build up) the person? Third, would my telling it please God?

The tenth commandment: "You shall not covet your neighbor's house; you shall not covet your neighbor's wife, nor his male servant, nor his female servant, nor his ox, nor his donkey, nor anything that is your neighbor's."

We must not have unholy desires for anything that belongs to our friends and neighbors. We should rejoice over the blessings of others and not envy their family, job, money, house, automobile, clothes, or anything they possess:

Delight yourself also in the Lord, and He shall give you the desires of your heart.

—PSALM 37:4

And having food and clothing, with these we shall be content. But those who desire to be rich fall into temptation and a snare, and into many foolish and harmful lusts which drown men in destruction and perdition. For the love of money is a root of all kinds of evil, for which some have strayed from the faith in their greediness, and pierced themselves through with many sorrows.

—1 TIMOTHY 6:8–10

A SUMMARY OF THE LAW

The first four commandments are referred to as the "first table of the Law." These four commandments deal with man's relationship to God. Jesus sums them up in these words:

Jesus said…"'You shall love the Lord your God with all your heart, with all your soul, and with all your mind.' This is the first and great commandment."

—MATTHEW 22:37–38

The last six commandments are referred to as the "second table of the Law." These commandments deal with man's relationship with his fellow man. Jesus sums them up with these words in Matthew 22:39, "And the second is like it: 'You shall love your neighbor as yourself.'"

Paul the Apostle gives us the summary of the whole Law in Romans 13:10, "Love does no harm to a neighbor; therefore love is the fulfillment of the law." If we truly love God and our fellow man, we will do what is right (righteous) toward God and man. When we break the Law, we are under a curse. However, no one can be saved and have eternal life by keeping the Law:

"Cursed is everyone who does not continue in all things which are written in the book of the law, to do them." But that no one is justified by the law in the sight of God is evident, for "the just shall live by faith."

—GALATIANS 3:10–11

God Kept His Covenant Word. What About Israel?

We have read in Exodus 19:5–6 how God reconfirmed His covenant with Israel, offering them a most glorious relationship; the sad thing is that Israel did not keep her part of the bargain. Israel broke the covenant with God many, many times. Finally, after multiplied failures, God announced His plan to end the old covenant with Israel. The words of the prophet Jeremiah reveal God's intentions. These are some of the most important words in all of the Old Testament (covenant). We call this the pivot point of God's dealings with Israel:

> Behold, the days are coming, says the Lord, when I will make a new covenant with the house of Israel and with the house of Judah—not according to the covenant that I made with their fathers in the day that I took them by the hand to lead them out of the land of Egypt, My covenant which they broke, though I was a husband to them, says the Lord. But this is the covenant that I will make with the house of Israel after those days, says the Lord: I will put My law in their minds, and write it on their hearts; and I will be their God, and they shall be My people. No more shall every man teach his neighbor, and every man his brother, saying, "Know the Lord," for they all shall know Me, from the least of them to the greatest of them, says the Lord. For I will forgive their iniquity, and their sin I will remember no more.
>
> —Jeremiah 31:31–34

Jesus and the New Covenant

What the prophet has described is the coming of the new covenant through the Lord Jesus Christ. We leave this lesson with grand words of revelation. The coming of Jesus to the world was not only going to be the end of the old covenant, but also its fulfillment. Everything promised comes to pass in the Messiah, the Christ:

> All of God's promises have been fulfilled in Him [Jesus]. Therefore, we say, "Amen" when we give glory to God through Christ [the Messiah].
>
> —2 Corinthians 1:20, author's paraphrase

Chapter 7

Israel: the Land, the Kingdom, and the Failures

AFTER ISRAEL LEFT Egypt, they came rather quickly to Mount Sinai (also called Mount Horeb, the place where Moses saw the burning bush), and it was here God gave them the Law. On the mount, God also gave Moses a plan to build a tabernacle. The tabernacle of Moses was to be God's dwelling place among His people. Not long afterwards, God brought them to the Jordan River, to a place called Kadesh Barnea, and He told them to go over and possess the land of Canaan. This was the land God had promised to Abraham and his descendants (Gen. 12:1, 7).

When they came to the Jordan, Moses reminded them of God's promise and gave them the following word:

> See, I have set the land before you; go in and possess the land which the Lord swore to your fathers—to Abraham, Isaac, and Jacob—to give to them and their descendants after them. [God was saying, "It is your land; go and get it."]
> —DEUTERONOMY 1:8

In Numbers 13, God instructed Moses to send twelve spies to the land of Canaan to investigate the land and the heathen people. These men were to come back with a battle strategy for Israel to defeat the enemy. Instead, ten of the spies came back with "a bad report," a report of fear and unbelief (Num. 13:32). They told all the reasons Israel could not go in and possess the land.

However, two of these men, Joshua and Caleb, came back with a different report. They said, "We are well able to overcome it" (Numbers 13:30). Unfortunately, the nation of Israel became fearful. The people accepted the report of unbelief and refused to enter into the land God had promised them. They were ready to choose a new leader to take them back to all the atrocities and bondage of Egypt.

When God saw their fear and their rebellion against Moses, He knew He could not use a people of unbelief and fear to go into battle. He caused them to turn back into the wilderness, where they wandered for forty years. Joshua and Caleb and those who were less than twenty years old would survive. All of the older people died in the forty years of wilderness wanderings.

ISRAEL GETS A SECOND CHANCE AND A NEW LEADER

The forty years of wanderings came to an end, and it was time for a change of leadership. Moses had one last blessing for Israel—and one last trip with God:

> Then Moses went up from the plains of Moab to Mount Nebo, to the top of Pisgah, which is across from Jericho. And the Lord showed him all the land…Then the Lord said to him, "This is the land of which I swore to give Abraham, Isaac, and Jacob, saying, 'I will give it to your descendants. I have caused you to see it with your eyes, but you shall not cross over there.'" So Moses the servant of the Lord died there in the land of Moab, according to the word of the Lord.
>
> —DEUTERONOMY 34:1, 4–5

Joshua now became the new leader of the nation of Israel. He was well qualified. He was one of the two spies who had come back from Canaan with a positive, faith report. He was God's choice and the choice of Moses:

> Now Joshua the son of Nun was full of the spirit of wisdom, for
> Moses had laid his hands on him; so the children of Israel heeded
> him, and did as the Lord had commanded Moses.
>
> —DEUTERONOMY 34:9

The story of Joshua receiving his commission from almighty God is an
exciting passage:

> After the death of Moses the servant of the Lord, it came to pass
> that the Lord spoke to Joshua the son of Nun, Moses' assistant,
> saying: "Moses My servant is dead. Now therefore, arise, go over
> this Jordan, you and all this people, to the land which I am giv-
> ing to them—the children of Israel. Every place that the sole of
> your foot will tread upon I have given you, as I said to Moses.
> From the wilderness and this Lebanon as far as the great river, the
> River Euphrates, all the land of the Hittites, and to the Great Sea
> toward the going down of the sun, shall be your territory. No man
> shall be able to stand before you all the days of your life; as I was
> with Moses, so I will be with you. I will not leave you nor forsake
> you. Be strong and of good courage, for to this people you shall
> divide as an inheritance the land which I swore to their fathers
> to give them. Only be strong and very courageous, that you may
> observe to do according to all the law which Moses My servant
> commanded you; do not turn from it to the right hand or to the
> left, that you may prosper wherever you go. This Book of the Law
> shall not depart from your mouth, but you shall meditate in it
> day and night, that you may observe to do according to all that
> is written in it. For then you will make your way prosperous, and
> then you will have good success."
>
> —JOSHUA 1:1–8

What a marvelous way to begin a new ministry, to start on a new job!
Joshua was a great leader, and he did bring them into their new land—
into the total inheritance that had been promised to them by God:

> So the Lord gave to Israel all the land of which He had sworn to
> give to their fathers, and they took possession of it and dwelt in it.
> The Lord gave them rest all around, according to all that He had
> sworn to their fathers. And not a man of all their enemies stood

against them; the Lord delivered all their enemies into their hand. Not a word failed of any good thing which the Lord had spoken to the house of Israel. All came to pass.

—JOSHUA 21:43–45

Joshua was a powerful leader. The Bible tells us, "Israel served the Lord all the days of Joshua, and all the days of the elders who outlived Joshua, who had known all the works of the Lord which He had done for Israel" (Josh. 24:31).

After the death of Joshua and his elders, the people of Israel sinned and began to worship the idols and false gods of the heathen nations around them. God's judgment quickly followed:

> Then the children of Israel did evil in the sight of the Lord, and served the Baals [false gods]; and they forsook the Lord God of their fathers, who had brought them out of the land of Egypt; and they followed other gods from among the gods of the people who were all around them, and they bowed down to them; and they provoked the Lord to anger... And the anger of the Lord was hot against Israel. So He delivered them into the hands of plunderers who despoiled them; and He sold them into the hands of their enemies all around, so that they could no longer stand before their enemies... Nevertheless, the Lord raised up judges who delivered them out of the hand of those who plundered them. Yet they would not listen to their judges, but they played the harlot with other gods, and bowed down to them. They turned quickly from the way in which their fathers walked, in obeying the commandments of the Lord; they did not do so.
>
> —JUDGES 2:11–12, 14, 16–17

This passage is most important, for it tells us that God now raised up leaders called "judges." These judges were to hear from God and lead the people of Israel. Sometimes they were good leaders; at other times, they were bad. There were fifteen judges, including Gideon, Samson, and Samuel. The last of the judges and the first in the line of the prophets, Samuel had a most unique position. He also served as a priest to Israel. First Samuel 3:20 says, "And all Israel... knew that Samuel had been established as a prophet of the Lord."

From Judges to Kings

Israel had a unique and wonderful relationship with God. He was to be their God, and they were to be His people. Yet they constantly rebelled against God and did not appreciate their unique relationship. They wanted to be like other (ungodly) nations. Their bad attitudes and unholy desires finally brought the period of the judges to a close. They asked for a king to rule over them:

> Then all the elders of Israel gathered together and came to Samuel at Ramah, and said to him, "Look, you are old, and your sons do not walk in your ways. Now make us a king to judge us like all the nations."
>
> —1 Samuel 8:4–5

This desire of the people did not please Samuel, and it did not please God. Samuel tried to change their minds, but it didn't work:

> But the thing displeased Samuel when they said, "Give us a king to judge us." So Samuel prayed to the Lord. And the Lord said to Samuel, "Heed the voice of the people in all that they say to you; for they have not rejected you, but they have rejected Me, that I should not reign over them".... Nevertheless the people refused to obey the voice of Samuel; and they said, "No, but we will have a king over us, that we also may be like all the nations, and that our king may judge us and go out before us and fight our battles."
>
> —1 Samuel 8:6–7, 19–20

So the rule of the judges ended with Samuel, and Saul became the first king of Israel:

> Then Samuel took a flask of oil and poured it on his [Saul's] head, and kissed him and said: "Is it not because the Lord has anointed you commander over His inheritance?"
>
> —1 Samuel 10:1

ISRAEL AND HER FIRST KING

The people were excited about their new king. In 1 Samuel 11:15, we learn that "all the people went to Gilgal, and there they made Saul king before the Lord." In the beginning of his reign, Saul walked with God. Later, he disobeyed the word God gave him through the prophet Samuel. He had been told to completely destroy an enemy nation, but he did not do it. He spared Agag, the king of that nation. No doubt he was trying to set a precedent that kings would be spared, even if their nations lost the battle. He also intruded into the office of the priesthood. Without any authority from God, he offered a sacrifice before the Lord. These stories are told in detail in 1 Samuel, chapters 13–15.

As a result of his disobedience, Saul lost out with God:

> But Samuel said to Saul..."you have rejected the word of the Lord, and the Lord has rejected you from being king over Israel."
> —1 SAMUEL 15:26

The Spirit of God departed from Saul, and when he could no longer hear from God, he consulted a witch in an attempt to hear from the dead prophet Samuel. First Samuel 31 tells us that Israel was defeated by the Philistine army, and Saul committed suicide.

DAVID: ISRAEL'S GREATEST KING

David was the young man chosen by God to become Israel's greatest king:

> Then Samuel took the horn of oil and anointed him in the midst of his brothers; and the Spirit of the Lord came upon David from that day forward.
> —1 SAMUEL 16:13

We know God had a special place in His heart for David. In 1 Samuel 13:14, God calls him "a man after His own heart." We know David was a mighty king and a great warrior, but the thing that impresses us most is David's relationship with God. He was the writer of the great majority of the psalms, which we not only read, but also put to music and sing in our times of praise and worship.

However, we cannot tell the complete story of David without discussing his awful sin. While the armies of Israel were out on the battlefield, David saw another man's wife and committed adultery with her. When the woman, Bathsheba, told David she was pregnant, the king caused her husband, Uriah, to be killed on the battlefield.

This shows us the power of sin! Even great leaders can be tempted and trapped by the devil. After Bathsheba's husband was murdered, David took her as his wife. The child produced by their unholy relationship died. In the middle of all these problems, David survived. God did not cast him away. The Bible gives us his secret of survival. He did not run from God, but he confessed his sins and turned to the Lord in worship:

> So David said to Nathan, "I have sinned against the Lord." And Nathan said to David, "The Lord also has put away your sin; you shall not die".... When David saw that his servants were whispering, David perceived that the child was dead. Therefore David said to his servants, "Is the child dead?" And they said, "He is dead." So David arose from the ground, washed and anointed himself, and changed his clothes; and he went into the house of the Lord and worshiped.
>
> —2 SAMUEL 12:13, 19–20

This is a tremendous example of God's mercy. David sinned, took another man's wife, and had that man killed. David suffered, but He was forgiven and restored. In 2 Samuel 7:16, God promised David his throne would be established forever. David's physical descendants failed God, and Israel had an awful record of failures. Yet, every promise of God was fulfilled through the person of Jesus, the Christ. He was the "Seed" of God—and of Abraham—to whom the promises were made. He was God's Son and David's Son. The words of the angel spoken to the Virgin Mary tell the story:

> Then the angel said to her, "Do not be afraid, Mary, for you have found favor with God. And behold, you will conceive in your womb and bring forth a Son, and shall call His name JESUS. He will be great, and will be called the Son of the Highest; and the Lord God will give Him the throne of His father David."
>
> —LUKE 1:30–32

Solomon: Israel's Third King

Solomon, the son of David and Bathsheba, became king after his father. God gave Solomon an awesome responsibility. He was to build a great temple. This temple, called "the temple of Solomon," was to be the house of God that would replace the tabernacle of Moses. Solomon accepted this assignment:

> And behold, I propose to build a house for the name of the Lord my God, as the Lord spoke to my father David, saying, "Your son, whom I will set on your throne in your place, he shall build the house for My name."
>
> —1 Kings 5:5

We can describe Solomon's relationship with God in the following three statements:

1. In the beginning, Solomon's walk was pleasing to the Lord; yet he was not perfect:

> And Solomon loved the Lord, walking in the statutes of his father David, except that he sacrificed and burned incense at the high places.
>
> —1 Kings 3:3

2. God allowed Solomon to complete the great temple:

> So all the work that King Solomon had done for the house of the Lord was finished; and Solomon brought in the things which his father David had dedicated: the silver and the gold and the furnishings. He put them in the treasuries of the house of the Lord.
>
> —1 Kings 7:51

3. The Lord showed His approval of Solomon's work by filling the temple with His glory:

> And it came to pass, when the priests came out of the holy place, that the cloud filled the house of the Lord, so that the priests could

not continue ministering because of the cloud; for the glory of the Lord filled the house of the Lord.

—1 KINGS 8:10–11

SOLOMON'S FAILURE . . . ISRAEL'S FAILURE

It is amazing but often true: like father like son. David's failure came because of a woman, Bathsheba, and Solomon's heart was turned from God by his heathen wives. Israel's wisest king was led into idolatry by the women in his life. The saddest thing about this story is that the people followed the king's bad example. If we have learned one thing about God, it is this: He will not tolerate idolatry. Judgment always follows idolatry:

> But if you or your sons at all turn from following Me, and do not keep My commandments and My statutes which I have set before you, but go and serve other gods and worship them, then I will cut off Israel from the land which I have given them; and this house which I have consecrated for My name I will cast out of My sight. Israel will be a proverb and a byword among all peoples.
>
> —1 KINGS 9:6–7

> For it was so, when Solomon was old, that his wives turned his heart after other gods; and his heart was not loyal to the Lord his God, as was the heart of his father David.
>
> —1 KINGS 11:4

Judgment certainly came upon both Solomon and Israel. God told Solomon He would take the kingdom from him (1 Kings 11:11–12). After Solomon's death, the kingdom was divided. The northern kingdom, with ten tribes, retained the name Israel and was ruled by Solomon's servant Jeroboam. The southern kingdom, with the two tribes of Judah and Benjamin, was named Judah and was ruled by Solomon's son, Rehoboam (1 Kings 11:31–32, 12:20).

The judgment became complete when King Nebuchadnezzar of Babylon sent his armies to conquer Jerusalem and destroy the temple:

He [Nebuchadnezzar's servant] burned the house of the Lord and the king's house; all the houses of Jerusalem, that is, all the houses of the great, he burned with fire.

—2 KINGS 25:9

From the time of its beginning until the time of its division, the whole kingdom of Israel lasted about 120 years. Saul reigned for forty years; David reigned for forty years; Solomon reigned for forty years (Acts 13:21; 2 Sam. 5:4; 1 Kings 11:42). Rehoboam reigned only a short time before the kingdom was split.

The divided kingdoms of Israel and Judah were both guilty of the sin of idolatry. They left the true and living God to worship other (false and lifeless) gods (2 Kings 17:15–16, 21:9). As a result, heathen armies came and took them captive. The Assyrians carried Israel captive into their land. The nation of Babylon conquered Judah and took it captive (2 Kings 17:20, 23:27). The captivity of Judah lasted seventy years (Jer. 25:11; 2 Chron. 36:21).

In closing this chapter, one thing is important to remember. Israel failed God many, many times, and great judgment came upon this nation. Nevertheless, the promises of God to Abraham, Isaac, and Jacob did not fail. When Israel went into the different captivities, only a small group came out of the captivity. This small group was known as the "remnant."

Although the promises of deliverance were given to the whole nation, only the remnant would believe the promises and be delivered. Jesus is the "remnant" of God. In Him the promises of God are fulfilled. He is the real "Seed" to whom the promises were made:

Now to Abraham and his Seed were the promises made. He does not say, "And to seeds," as of many, but as of one, "And to your Seed," who is Christ.

—GALATIANS 3:16

Chapter 8

THE PROPHETS

THE WORD *PROPHET* is used over 240 times in the Bible. Two words are translated "prophet." One, *nabiy* (pronounced "naw-bee") is a Hebrew word used in the Old Testament. The other, *prophetes* (pronounced "prof-ay'-tace") is from the Greek language and is used in the New Testament.

The general meaning of the word *prophet* is "one who is inspired, a foreteller, an inspired speaker." In the Bible, it specifically refers to "one who speaks on behalf of God." The prophets were not to speak their own words, but God's words to the people:

> For prophecy never came by the will of man, but holy men of God spoke as they were moved by the Holy Spirit.
> —2 PETER 1:21

The word *moved* means a "rushing, driving force." This prophetic ministry can also be expressed as being "energized" by the Holy Spirit. The minds of the prophets were given understanding, and they were "moved" to speak the words of God to the people. None of this means the prophets were irresponsible or without control of their faculties. At times, they prophesied in song and with musical instruments. Samuel the prophet anointed Saul to be the first king of Israel. Then, he gave him these words:

> You will meet a group of prophets coming down from the high place with a stringed instrument, a tambourine, a flute, and a harp before them; and they will be prophesying. Then the Spirit of the Lord will come upon you, and you will prophesy with them and be turned into another man.
>
> —1 SAMUEL 10:5–6

In 1 Chronicles 25:1, the Bible speaks of men who would prophesy with musical instruments.

Sixteen men wrote seventeen books of prophecy in the Old Testament. We divide them into two categories—major prophets and minor prophets. This does not mean some were more important than others. Major prophets wrote more; minor prophets wrote less.

The four major prophets were: Isaiah, Jeremiah (who also wrote the Book of Lamentations), Ezekiel, and Daniel. The twelve minor prophets were: Hosea, Joel, Amos, Obadiah, Jonah, Micah, Nahum, Habakkuk, Zephaniah, Haggai, Zechariah, and Malachi.

In this chapter, we will deal mainly with the Old Testament prophets and their prophecies. Later, when we study about the new covenant, we will learn about the prophetic ministry that is available to us today. The new covenant was made with Israel and came into existence as a result of the death, burial, and resurrection of Jesus. On the Day of Pentecost, with the outpouring of the Holy Spirit, this covenant was put into full operation.

One of the most important things about prophecy is this: the Holy Spirit is the author of prophecy, so He has to be the explainer of the prophecy:

> Knowing this first, that no prophecy of Scripture is of any private interpretation [not our own personal interpretation], for prophecy never came by the will of man, but holy men of God spoke as they were moved by the Holy Spirit.
>
> —2 PETER 1:20–21

Today, the Holy Spirit within us will help us understand what the Holy Spirit in the prophets caused them to speak and write.

We can trust the message of the Bible prophets for two reasons. First, much of it has already happened. Second, the rest of it is happening right now, all around us. Here are some examples of prophecy being fulfilled. In Jeremiah 25:11, the prophet said the people of God would be in Babylonian captivity for seventy years. Here is the prophecy:

> And this whole land shall be a desolation and an astonishment, and these nations shall serve the king of Babylon seventy years.
> —JEREMIAH 25:11

Here is the fulfillment:

> And those who escaped from the sword he [Nebuchadnezzar] carried away to Babylon, where they became servants to him and his sons until the rule of the kingdom of Persia, to fulfill the word of the Lord by the mouth of Jeremiah, until the land had enjoyed her Sabbaths. As long as she lay desolate she kept Sabbath, to fulfill seventy years.
> —2 CHRONICLES 36:20–21

Another example comes from the prophet Joel. He prophesied in Joel 2:28 that the day would come when God would pour out His Spirit on all flesh. This outpouring happened on the Day of Pentecost:

> But Peter, standing up with the eleven, raised his voice and said to them, "Men of Judea and all who dwell in Jerusalem, let this be known to you, and heed my words"… this is what was spoken by the prophet Joel.
> —ACTS 2:14, 16

In verse 22 he calls them "men of Israel." The remnant to whom he was speaking represented both Israel and Judah.

The Bible tells us in Acts 3:19–21 that Jesus will not return until the words of God's prophets have been fulfilled.

THE MINISTRY, MISSION, AND MESSAGE OF THE PROPHETS

The ministry, mission, and message of the prophets had one great purpose: to turn the nations of Israel and Judah from their sin, their idolatry, and rebellion against God, and bring them back to God. This objective can be summed up in the following scripture:

> And the Lord has sent to you all His servants the prophets, rising early and sending them but you have not listened nor inclined your ear to hear. They said, "Repent now everyone of his evil way and his evil doings, and dwell in the land that the Lord has given to you and your fathers forever and ever. Do not go after other gods to serve them and worship them, and do not provoke Me to anger with the works of your hands; and I will not harm you."
>
> —JEREMIAH 25:4–6

The message (as shown in Isa. 1:16, 18; Ezek. 18:30; and Jer. 23:3) was usually presented in three steps:

1. Israel and Judah were warned to turn from their evil ways and come back to God.

2. Judgment (captivity) would come on all who did not repent (turn to God).

3. After the judgment, a small group (the remnant) would be delivered out of their captivity.

THE MESSAGE OF THE PROPHETS CONCERNING JESUS, THE CHRIST—MESSIAH

We Christians can greatly rejoice in the way the prophecies about Jesus were fulfilled. He did not just show up. He came to fulfill in great detail the prophetic Word of God. As we read the prophecies, we learn many valuable things. This Savior (Redeemer) would come from the family of King David. He would suffer and die for them, saving them from their sins:

> "Behold, the days are coming," says the Lord, "That I will raise to David a Branch of righteousness; a King shall reign and prosper, and execute judgment and righteousness in the earth. In His days Judah will be saved, and Israel will dwell safely; now this is His name by which He will be called: THE LORD OUR RIGHTEOUSNESS."
>
> —JEREMIAH 23:5–6

In those days and at that time I will cause to grow up to David a Branch of righteousness; He shall execute judgment and righteousness in the earth.

—JEREMIAH 33:15

But He was wounded for our transgressions, He was bruised for our iniquities; the chastisement for our peace was upon Him, and by His stripes we are healed.

—ISAIAH 53:5

In that day a fountain shall be opened for the house of David and for the inhabitants of Jerusalem, for sin and for uncleanness.

—ZECHARIAH 13:1

One of the great messages of the prophets was the new covenant that God was going to make with His people. The pivot point of the Old Testament is found in Jeremiah 31. Here, God explains the total failure of Israel under the old covenant and gives His plans for their future:

"Behold, the days are coming, says the Lord, when I will make a new covenant with the house of Israel and with the house of Judah—not according to the covenant that I made with their fathers in the day that I took them by the hand to lead them out of the land of Egypt, My covenant which they broke, though I was a husband to them, says the Lord. But this is the covenant that I will make with the house of Israel after those days, says the Lord: I will put My law in their minds, and write it on their hearts; and I will be their God, and they shall be My people. No more shall every man teach his neighbor, and every man his brother, saying, 'Know the Lord,' for they all shall know Me, from the least of them to the greatest of them, says the Lord. For I will forgive their iniquity, and their sin I will remember no more."

—JEREMIAH 31:31–34

In this new covenant, all racial barriers would be broken down. Jews and Gentiles—all people—would come through the same door of salvation. Jesus is this door:

For behold, the darkness shall cover the earth, and deep darkness the people; but the Lord will arise over you, and His glory will be seen upon you. The Gentiles shall come to your light, and kings to the brightness of your rising.

—ISAIAH 60:2–3

JESUS: THE KINGDOM AND THE CHURCH

The kingdom of God has always existed. Where God is manifested, He is in charge. He rules. God's kingdom existed in the Garden of Eden, on Noah's ark, and in the nation of Israel. The Old Testament prophets told of a time when Jesus would set up His kingdom, and through His church He would bring a great restoration to the people of God.

Later we will study about the kingdom of God in detail, but for now we will only introduce the idea. It is our hope that this will produce some excitement and anticipation for our future chapters. Remember that Jesus was born, lived, died, was resurrected, and ascended to heaven during the time of the Roman Empire. Kings called "Caesar" ruled the empire:

And in the days of these kings [the Caesars] the God of heaven will set up a kingdom which shall never be destroyed; and the kingdom shall not be left to other people; it shall break in pieces and consume all these kingdoms, and it shall stand forever.

—DANIEL 2:44

THE ARK OF GOD'S PRESENCE

Before we go any further, we must tell about a strange thing that happened when David became king. You will remember that Moses, with the instructions God gave him on Mount Sinai, had created a tabernacle. In this tabernacle was a box called "the ark of the covenant." This ark was made of plain wood and covered with pure gold. On the top of the lid over the ark, a golden angelic creature was carved on each end. God had promised Moses that He would come and live among His people. He manifested His presence above this lid, between these two creatures called "cherubim" (Exod. 25:18–22).

However, during a time of Israel's rebellion against God, they worshiped idols and lived in gross sin. An enemy nation—the Philistines— came against them, defeated them, and took the ark back to their land.

God caused the ark to become a source of great trouble to the Philistines, and they sent it back to a place close to Jerusalem. The ark stayed there through the reign of King Saul, but when David became king, he brought it back to Jerusalem.

Here is the surprising thing: David did not take the ark back to the tabernacle of Moses. Instead, he built a small "tent-tabernacle" and placed the ark in it. David would stand before the ark, lift his hands to God, and offer praise and worship to the Lord. Instead of blood sacrifice, David would offer the sacrifice of praise to God. He was, like Jesus, a prophet, priest, and king. It seems that after the initial animal sacrifices were made, they continued by offering praise and worship as their main sacrifices to God before the ark. Blood sacrifices continued in Gibeon at the site of the tabernacle of Moses.

When David died, Solomon became king and built a great temple. He brought the ark of the covenant into the temple, where it was seen only once each year by the high priest. Israel always looked back to the time of David and to the "tabernacle of David" as the golden years of blessing. Little did they know at the time, but this tabernacle of David was a symbol and type of the church that Jesus would build.

The prophet Amos prophesied these words in Amos 9:11:

> On that day I will raise up the tabernacle of David, which has fallen down, and repair its damages; I will raise up its ruins, and rebuild it as in the days of old.

But what does this mean? We find our answer in the New Testament. The disciples in Jerusalem were trying to settle the question about Gentiles coming into the church, which had been exclusively Jewish. Here is the word God gave to them:

> Simon [Peter] has declared how God at the first visited the Gentiles to take out of them a people for His name. And with this the words of the prophets agree, just as it is written: "After this I will return and will rebuild the tabernacle of David, which has fallen down; I will rebuild its ruins, and I will set it up; so that the rest of mankind may seek the Lord, Even all the Gentiles who are called by My name, says the Lord who does all these things."
>
> —ACTS 15:14–17

THE PLACE OF GOD'S PRESENCE

- First, the ark and the presence of God were in the tabernacle of Moses.

- Then, the ark and the presence of God were in the most unusual tabernacle of David.

- Next, the ark was in the temple of Solomon.

- Finally, today, the presence of God is not in a building, not identified with a box. The presence of God is in His people, the church.

Many of the prophets spoke about the glorious things that were going to happen in the future, and they were speaking of God's blessing upon the church, the tabernacle of David that was to be restored (Jer. 23:3–4, 33:11; Hab. 2:14).

1. Ministry gifts were to be given, and true shepherds would love and feed the people of God.

2. There would be the restoration of pure sacrifices of praise and worship.

3. Through the church, the earth would be filled with the knowledge of the glory of God.

We have used only a few pages to tell you about the great prophets of God in the Old Testament. Soon, we will be studying about Jesus, about the new covenant, about our great salvation, and about the church Jesus built. When we study about the church, we will find that prophets still exist in the world today and that these prophets still speak the word of God to His people. We have exciting times ahead!

Chapter 9

THE RESTORATION
OF ISRAEL

MANY PEOPLE BELIEVE the Bible is the story of mankind search-ing for God, stumbling toward His will for their lives. This is a false concept. The Bible is really the story of God reaching out in love to His creation, revealing Himself to humanity, wanting to have fellowship and a relationship with the people He made.

When God called Abraham, He established a covenant with him. This covenant set the rules for the relationship God wanted to have, not just with Abraham, but with a whole nation of people that was to come from him. This nation was Israel.

The record of the Bible is the story of man running from God, rebelling against God, and even turning from Him to worship idols. As a result of this sinful conduct, God allowed Israel's enemies to come and plunder its land, kill its leaders and take many of the people captive. Often the enemy nations took the "cream of the crop"—the nobility, the strongest, and the wisest, especially the youth—to their lands.

We have already learned how Israel was divided shortly after the death of Solomon, King David's son. The ten northern tribes retained the name

Israel, and the two southern tribes of Judah and Benjamin took the name Judah.

The northern kingdom of Israel survived as a nation for about two hundred years. Then, in approximately 720 B.C. (before Christ), Israel was conquered and taken captive by the nation of Assyria. Judah, the southern kingdom, lasted a little longer, but in about 586 B.C. the armies of Babylon came into its land, plundered the temple of Solomon, and took many of the people to Babylon. Nebuchadnezzar, the king of Babylon, was probably the most totalitarian ruler we find in the Bible. Both the Assyrian and Babylonian captivities took place over a period of years.

During this time, the prophets Daniel and Ezekiel were taken captive. Ultimately, Jerusalem was destroyed, and all but the poorest people were taken away. We must establish and understand one important fact. All of Israel did not go into the Assyrian captivity, and all of Judah did not go into the captivity of Babylon. Some were left in their land. Most of those who were left bowed to their conquerors and forgot their spiritual heritage.

CYRUS AND THE REMNANT

The nation of Babylon was later conquered by the Medes and Persians. They had a ruler by the name of Cyrus, and here is one of the great miracles of the Bible. Two hundred years before Cyrus was born, the prophet Isaiah spoke about him:

> [Cyrus] is My shepherd, and he shall perform all My pleasure, saying to Jerusalem, "You shall be built," and to the temple, "Your foundation shall be laid."
>
> —ISAIAH 44:28

> Thus says the Lord to His anointed, to Cyrus, whose right hand I have held—to subdue nations before him and loose the armor of kings, to open before him the double doors, so that the gates will not be shut...I will give you the treasures of darkness and hidden riches of secret places, that you may know that I, the Lord, who call you by your name, am the God of Israel. For Jacob My servant's sake, and Israel My elect, I have even called you by your name; I have named you, though you have not known Me.
>
> —ISAIAH 45:1, 3–4

When Cyrus came along, he certainly understood that the hand of God was upon him:

> Now in the first year of Cyrus king of Persia, that the word of the Lord by the mouth of Jeremiah might be fulfilled, the Lord stirred up the spirit of Cyrus king of Persia, so that he made a proclamation throughout all his kingdom, and also put it in writing, saying,
>
> Thus says Cyrus king of Persia: All the kingdoms of the earth the Lord God of heaven has given me. And He has commanded me to build Him a house at Jerusalem which is in Judah.
>
> Who is among you of all His people? May his God be with him, and let him go up to Jerusalem which is in Judah, and build the house of the Lord God of Israel [He is God], which is in Jerusalem.
>
> And whoever is left in any place where he dwells, let the men of his place help him with silver and gold, with goods and livestock, besides the freewill offerings for the house of God which is in Jerusalem.
>
> —EZRA 1:1–4

THE REMNANT PRINCIPLE

All of this activity illustrates what we call the "remnant principle." A great number of Jews were carried captive to Babylon. Only about fifty thousand returned to build the temple. How true are these words of Isaiah 1:9:

> Unless the Lord of hosts had left to us a very small remnant, we would have become like Sodom, we would have been made like Gomorrah.

The remnant principle can be stated in a few words: "God would give promises to the whole nation of Israel. The majority of the people (and the leaders) would rebel against God with unbelief, often going into sinful practices, especially idolatry. God would then bring judgment on this rebellious majority, but He would fulfill His promises to the small, believing group that was left. This group was known as the remnant."

In the Book of Romans, Paul tells the story of Israel's failure. Notice how he interprets the true meaning of the word *remnant* as meaning "seed." There can be no doubt that this "Seed" is the Lord Jesus Christ, the one to whom the promises of God were ultimately made (Gal. 3:16):

> And as Isaiah said before: "Unless the Lord of Sabaoth had left us a seed, we would have become like Sodom, and we would have been made like Gomorrah." What shall we say then? That Gentiles, who did not pursue righteousness, have attained to righteousness, even the righteousness of faith; but Israel, pursuing the law of righteousness, has not attained to the law of righteousness. Why? Because they did not seek it by faith, but as it were, by the works of the law. For they stumbled at that stumbling stone. [This is Jesus.] As it is written: "Behold, I lay in Zion a stumbling stone and rock of offense, And whoever believes on Him will not be put to shame."
>
> —ROMANS 9:29–33

This stone was a "Him"—Jesus!

God made many promises to the whole nation of Israel. Yet, over and over, the overwhelming majority failed to receive, believe, and act on the promises. Their sinful, rebellious conduct and their lack of faith in God and His Word caused God to send judgment rather than blessing.

Nevertheless, a small part out of the nation believed God. They called on the name of the Lord, asking forgiveness for themselves and the nation. God heard and answered their prayers, and this small group, the remnant, inherited the promises of God.

THE LEADERS OF THE REMNANT

Most of the information we have about the return of the remnant to Jerusalem is found in the Books of Ezra, Nehemiah, and Zechariah. These men were prominent in the return of the people to Jerusalem and as leaders in the job of rebuilding:

1. Zerubbabel was the governor during the rebuilding of the temple from about 535–515 B.C. He was also the grandson of King Jehoachin (Jeconiah), who had been carried captive to Babylon. This makes him a direct representative of David's family (Zech. 4:9).

2. Joshua was a most unusual man—a priest who was crowned. He represents the merging of the offices of high priest and king, which would be fulfilled in Jesus, the Christ:

Take the silver and gold, make an elaborate crown, and set it on the head of Joshua the son of Jehozadak, the high priest. Then speak to him, saying, "Thus says the Lord of hosts, saying: 'Behold, the Man whose name is the BRANCH! From His place He shall branch out, and He shall build the temple of the Lord; yes, He shall build the temple of the Lord. He shall bear the glory, and shall sit and rule on His throne; so He shall be a priest on His throne, and the counsel of peace shall be between them both.'"

—ZECHARIAH 6:11–13

3. Haggai and Zechariah were two of the prophets whose words of prophecy encouraged the people to finish the temple:

Then the prophet Haggai and Zechariah the son of Iddo, prophets, prophesied to the Jews who were in Judah and Jerusalem, in the name of the God of Israel, who was over them. So Zerubbabel the son of Shealtiel and Jeshua the son of Jozadak rose up and began to build the house of God which is in Jerusalem; and the prophets of God were with them, helping them.

—EZRA 5:1–2

So the elders of the Jews built, and they prospered through the prophesying of Haggai the prophet and Zechariah the son of Iddo. And they built and finished it, according to the commandment of the God of Israel, and according to the command of Cyrus, Darius, and Artaxerxes king of Persia.

—EZRA 6:14

4. Ezra was a scribe (one who copied the Scriptures) and a priest (Ezra 7:1–6).

5. Nehemiah was the cupbearer (the most trusted servant) of the king of Persia. He returned to Jerusalem about 445 B.C. with the job of restoring the walls of the city (Neh. 2:8).

The Temple and Walls Are Finished

All this work of restoration continued for many, many years. The important thing is this: in spite of all the opposition from their enemies, the people of the remnant finished their assignments. Both the temple and the walls of the city of Jerusalem were finished.

The kind of opposition the people faced when they were restoring the walls is the same kind of opposition the people of God face today on many fronts. This opposition was from two directions: (1) hindrance from their enemies without (the ungodly, heathen crowd), and (2) hindrance from within (from their own negative and unbelieving people). The majority of those in captivity did not want to return to their land and rebuild.

The enemies from without first tried scorn and ridicule, but this did not stop the people of the remnant:

> But it so happened, when Sanballat heard that we were rebuilding the wall, that he was furious and very indignant, and mocked the Jews....So we built the wall, and the entire wall was joined together up to half its height, for the people had a mind to work.
>
> —Nehemiah 4:1, 6

The enemy from without then threatened force, but this did not work:

> Those who built on the wall, and those who carried burdens, loaded themselves so that with one hand they worked at construction, and with the other held a weapon.
>
> —Nehemiah 4:17

God's Ultimate Remnant

In all of our Bible study, in all our reading of history, let us never lose sight of this important fact: "God's ultimate remnant was and is Jesus!" Do not ever lose hope when you read of the failures of the remnant that came back from Babylon. God's main purpose in bringing the Jews back to their homeland was to preserve the genealogical line of David until the "King" would be born.

Nathan the prophet gave this promise to David in 2 Samuel 7:16: "And your house and your kingdom shall be established forever before you. Your throne shall be established forever." The prophet Isaiah spoke these words concerning the coming of the Messiah:

> For unto us a Child is born, unto us a Son is given; and the government will be upon His shoulder. And His name will be called Wonderful, Counselor, Mighty God, Everlasting Father, Prince of Peace. Of the increase of His government and peace there will be no end, upon the throne of David and over His kingdom, to order it and establish it with judgment and justice from that time forward, even forever. The zeal of the Lord of hosts will perform this.
>
> —Isaiah 9:6–7

The fulfillment of these words comes in Luke 1:32–33:

> He will be great, and will be called the Son of the Highest; and the Lord God will give Him the throne of His father David. And He will reign over the house of Jacob forever, and of His kingdom there will be no end.

Paul the Apostle makes all of this very clear in Galatians 3:16: "Now to Abraham and his Seed were the promises made. He does not say, 'And to seeds,' as of many, but as of one, 'And to your Seed,' who is Christ."

THE INTERTESTAMENTAL PERIOD

The time between the ending of the Old Testament and the beginning of the New Testament was about four hundred years. During this time, different nations rose to power and ruled over Israel. The four nations that ruled over God's rebellious people were:

1. *Babylon*: With its leader Nebuchadnezzar, the most totalitarian nation depicted in the Bible.

2. *The Medo-Persian Empire*: Its leader Cyrus was greatly used by God. The Persians conquered the Medes and had the rule when this intertestamental period began.

3. *The Greek (Hellenistic) Empire*: Ruled by Alexander the Great. When he died, his empire was splintered among his generals. During this time, the Greek language was spread over the world.

4. *The Roman Empire*: Ruled by the Caesars, this empire started with the city of Rome defeating other cities and areas until it grew into a mighty force.

During the time of the intertestamental period, the people of Judah rebelled against the weakened Greek armies and gained their freedom. This did not last very long, and soon Rome came in and took over. When the New Testament opens, the people of Israel are under the authority of the Romans. The Roman domination lasted for hundreds of years.

During the four hundred years between the Old and the New Testaments, most of the people of Israel and Judah practiced a form of religion, but they had lost their faith in God's promises that dealt with the coming of the Messiah. But there was a group of people who never gave up. They never stopped believing that redemption was coming to Israel. They still believed God. They were still looking for the Messiah.

We close this chapter and this old covenant period with some thought-provoking questions: How is God going to reawaken these people? How is He going to get them back on track? We shall have the answers to these questions very soon. We will give you a hint. God is going to find for Himself a remnant. This remnant is going to change the world forever!

Chapter 10

Jesus,
the Christ—the Messiah

J ESUS WAS—AND IS—ONE of a kind! There was never anyone like Him before He was born of a virgin in Bethlehem; there has never been another like Him since that time. The prophet Isaiah spoke about Him:

> Therefore the Lord Himself will give you a sign: Behold, the virgin shall conceive and bear a Son, and shall call His name Immanuel.
> —Isaiah 7:14

Some have claimed that Jesus was merely a great man, but only the product of evolution rising to its highest form. This cannot be true. The claim of evolution is that the species is always going from the lower form to the higher. Therefore, if Jesus were the product of evolution, why has there not been another like Him or one even better?

We could waste our time answering many foolish questions and accusations about Jesus, but the truth is this—He is the Son of God. He is Deity. He is God come in the flesh! The Old Testament prophets had foretold His coming into the world. Even beginning in the Garden of Eden,

God had spoken these words to the serpent (Satan):

> And I will put enmity between you and the woman, and between your seed and her seed; He shall bruise your head, and you shall bruise His heel.
>
> —GENESIS 3:15

This happened when Jesus died on the cross, was buried, and rose again. There, He defeated sin, death, and Satan. As we continue studying about Jesus, we will see how often and how completely He fulfills the prophetic words spoken about Him in the Old Testament.

JESUS: THE MINISTER OF THE NEW COVENANT

When we studied about the old covenant, we found a portion of Scripture that we called the "pivot point" of that covenant. It was the point in history where God gave the prophetic promise concerning the new covenant He was going to make with Israel and Judah. They had failed God so often, their sinful rebellion had been so awful, and they had even begun to worship idols. God knew something else had to be done. Here is the way God describes His plan:

> Behold, the days are coming, says the Lord, when I will make a new covenant with the house of Israel and with the house of Judah—not according to the covenant that I made with their fathers in the day that I took them by the hand to lead them out of the land of Egypt, My covenant which they broke, though I was a husband to them, says the Lord. But this is the covenant that I will make with the house of Israel after those days, says the Lord: I will put My law in their minds, and write it on their hearts; and I will be their God, and they shall be My people.
>
> —JEREMIAH 31:31–33

In Ezekiel 16:60, God promised this would be "an everlasting covenant." God made it clear that He had been faithful to Israel. He had kept His covenant promises and agreements. He likened it to a marriage relationship. So when Israel went after other gods, they were committing spiritual adultery. Finally God said, "It's over, finished, hopeless, and done."

We learned about the old covenant God made with Abraham; now we must define the new covenant. The new covenant was the agreement or contract God made with Judah and Israel through the person of the Lord Jesus Christ. He was to be the "Key" who would make the new covenant work because He is the Mediator, the go-between in this covenant. His assignment was to reconcile mankind to God. Notice how definitely the Scriptures prove this idea:

> For there is one God and one Mediator between God and men, the Man Christ Jesus.
>
> —1 TIMOTHY 2:5

> But now He has obtained a more excellent ministry, inasmuch as He is also Mediator of a better covenant, which was established on better promises.
>
> —HEBREWS 8:6

> And for this reason He is the Mediator of the new covenant, by means of death, for the redemption of the transgressions under the first covenant, that those who are called may receive the promise of the eternal inheritance.
>
> —HEBREWS 9:15

> But you have come to Mount Zion...the heavenly Jerusalem...to the general assembly and church of the firstborn...to Jesus the Mediator of the new covenant.
>
> —HEBREWS 12:22–24

THE BLOOD OF THE NEW COVENANT

When the old covenant came into existence, it required the shedding of blood to ratify the covenant relationship between God and man. The new covenant had the same blood requirement, but there was a major difference. Under the old covenant, the people brought an animal sacrifice once each year. This sacrifice only delayed the penalty of sin for one year and could never forgive sins.

In contrast, the blood of the new covenant was shed only one time, and this blood will forgive sins forever! We might wonder how such a thing could happen, and here is the answer—the blood that binds, ratifies, and guarantees this new covenant is the blood of the Lord Jesus Christ:

Then He took the cup [at the Last Supper], and when He had given thanks He gave it to them, and they all drank from it. And He said to them, "This is My blood of the new covenant, which is shed for many."

—MARK 14:23–24

But Christ…with His own blood He entered the Most Holy Place once for all, having obtained eternal redemption [for us]. For if the blood of bulls and goats and the ashes of a heifer, sprinkling the unclean, sanctifies for the purifying of the flesh, how much more shall the blood of Christ, who through the eternal Spirit offered Himself without spot to God, cleanse your conscience from dead works to serve the living God?

—HEBREWS 9:11–14

We have been sanctified through the offering of the body of Jesus Christ once for all. [No blood sacrifice of any kind will ever have to be made again.]

—HEBREWS 10:10

WHAT HAPPENED TO THE OLD COVENANT?

Many have wondered: Is the old covenant gone? Will it ever return? Yes, it is gone. No, it will never return. There are three reasons for this:

1. The old covenant was abolished because of Israel's inability to keep its part of the covenant agreement:

For if that first covenant had been faultless, then no place would have been sought for a second. Because finding fault with them, He says: "Behold, the days are coming, says the Lord, when I will make a new covenant with the house of Israel and with the house of Judah."

—HEBREWS 8:7–8

2. The animal blood of the old covenant was powerless to take away sins:

For it is not possible that the blood of bulls and goats could take away sins.

—HEBREWS 10:4

3. The new covenant fulfills the purpose of God—the forgiveness of sins:

"How much more shall the blood of Christ...cleanse your conscience from dead works to serve the living God? And for this reason He is the Mediator...[and] now, once at the end of the ages, He has appeared to put away sin by the sacrifice of Himself."

—HEBREWS 9:14–15, 26

THE STORY OF THE NEW TESTAMENT

The New Testament is the second part of the Bible and contains four major divisions:

1. The Gospels (Matthew, Mark, Luke, and John) are the record of our Lord Jesus Christ—His birth, life, ministry, death, burial, resurrection, and ascension.

2. The Book of Acts is the historical account of the Church of Jesus Christ—its beginning and early years of growth.

3. The Epistles (letters) were written by the apostles and other holy men of God and addressed to the various churches and church groups they (and others) had planted. Some letters are written to specific churches; others are general Epistles. Some are written to individuals. All of them have one thing in common. They contain the teaching of valuable doctrine, and they are written to educate, regulate, and correct the conduct of the church and individuals in the church.

4. The Book of Revelation is "The Revelation of Jesus Christ." It is the history of the church and civilization, written before it happens. It is the story of Satan's attacks against the church and his efforts to frustrate God's purposes on the earth.

It ends with the triumph of the church over the devil, his demons, and all the powers of darkness.

THERE IS NO CHRISTIANITY WITHOUT JESUS!

In man-made religions, the leaders rise up, gather a following, live their lives, and die. For them, that is the end. Some of their teachings and philosophy may survive, but it is of no eternal value. Christianity is different. Without Jesus living, dying, buried, raised from the dead, ascended, and sitting at the "right hand of the majesty on high," there is no Christianity (Heb. 1:1–4). The strength of the Christian faith depends on the person of the resurrected Jesus Christ.

The beautiful message of Jesus is the message of salvation. We Christians claim there is no other way to receive God's salvation and eternal life except through faith in Jesus Christ. The Bible clearly confirms this to be true:

> For God so loved the world that He gave His only begotten Son, that whoever believes in Him should not perish but have everlasting life. For God did not send His Son into the world to condemn the world, but that the world through Him might be saved.
>
> —JOHN 3:16–17

> Let it be known to you all, and to all the people of Israel, that by the name of Jesus Christ of Nazareth, whom you crucified, whom God raised from the dead, by Him this man stands here before you whole.... Nor is there salvation in any other, for there is no other name under heaven given among men by which we must be saved.
>
> —ACTS 4:10, 12

HOW THEN DO WE DESCRIBE THIS ONE NAMED JESUS?

- This God-Man was called Jesus, which means "Savior," "Liberator," or "Deliverer":

> And she will bring forth a Son, and you shall call His name JESUS, for He will save His people from their sins.
>
> —MATTHEW 1:21

Salvation happens when Jesus forgives us of all our sins. Jesus said to a sinful woman, "Your sins are forgiven" (Luke 7:48). A man was brought to Jesus for healing, but Jesus took care of the sin problem first. "He said to the paralytic, 'Son, your sins are forgiven you'" (Mark 2:5).

- He is called *Christ*, coming from the Greek word, and *Messiah*, coming from the Hebrew. Both of these mean "the Anointed One." Jesus was certainly anointed. The Bible tells us that God's Spirit was upon him without measure or limit (John 3:34).

- Jesus is the Son of God and the son of Mary, truly God and truly man, and the only Mediator (go-between) who can represent both God and man. This Mediator was the only hope of reconciling (repairing the breach between) God and man:

Now all things are of God, who has reconciled us to Himself through Jesus Christ, and has given us the ministry of reconciliation.

—2 CORINTHIANS 5:18

It is beautiful to see this "God-Man" concept in the Scriptures:

And the angel answered and said to her, "The Holy Spirit will come upon you, and the power of the Highest will overshadow you; therefore, also, that Holy One who is to be born will be called the Son of God."

—LUKE 1:35

For in Him dwells all the fullness of the Godhead bodily.

—COLOSSIANS 2:9

For there is one God and one Mediator between God and men, the Man Christ Jesus.

—1 TIMOTHY 2:5

Many cults do not believe in the deity of our Lord Jesus, but the Bible boldly proclaims it. The prophet Isaiah described Him with these words in Isaiah 9:6:

For unto us a Child is born, Unto us a Son is given; and the government will be upon His shoulder. And His name will be called Wonderful, Counselor, Mighty God, Everlasting Father, Prince of Peace. [See also Hebrews 1:8]

The apostle John answered the call of Jesus. He walked with Him, saw the miracles, witnessed the crucifixion, and saw Him in bodily form after the Resurrection. This is his personal, God-inspired testimony about the Lord:

In the beginning was the Word, and the Word was with God, and the Word was God. He was in the beginning with God. All things were made through Him, and without Him nothing was made that was made...And the Word [God] became flesh and dwelt among us, and we beheld His glory, the glory as of the only begotten of the Father, full of grace and truth.

—John 1:1–3, 14

The apostle Paul saw Jesus in divine revelation on the road to Damascus. He wrote to Timothy, his son in the gospel, with this proclamation in 1 Timothy 3:16:

And without controversy great is the mystery of godliness: God [Greek word *theos*] was manifested in the flesh, justified in the Spirit, seen by angels, preached among the Gentiles, believed on in the world, received up in glory. [Jesus is the only possible person who fits this description.]

The Divine Attributes of Our Lord Jesus

The same divine attributes (special qualities and abilities) that are used to describe almighty God also apply to Jesus. He is:

- *Omnipotent* (all-powerful): Jesus proclaimed, "All authority [Greek word *exousia* meaning "authority, jurisdiction, strength, and power] has been given to Me in heaven and on earth" (Matt. 28:18).

- *Omniscient* (all-knowing): The disciples said to Jesus, "Now we are sure that You know all things…By this we believe that You came forth from God" (John 16:30).

- *Omnipresent* (everywhere present): Jesus made this promise, "For where two or three are gathered together in My name, I am there in the midst of them" (Matt. 18:20).

- *Eternal* (ever-existing—past, present, and future): "In the beginning was the Word, and the Word was with God, and the Word was God. He was in the beginning with God" (John 1:1–2). "Jesus said to them, 'Most assuredly, I say to you, before Abraham was, I AM'" (John 8:58).

WHY WAS ALL THIS "JESUS, GOD, AND MAN" NECESSARY?

In one of E. Stanley Jones's little devotion books, he tells this story. In a Sunday school class a teacher asked her students, "Who is Jesus Christ?" one student answered, "He's the best picture God ever took." This answer is profound. In Jesus, God fully revealed Himself, especially His love. Paul gives us this insight:

> But when the fullness of the time had come, God sent forth His Son, born of a woman, born under the law, to redeem those who were under the law, that we might receive the adoption as sons.
> —GALATIANS 4:4–5

Jesus, our Savior, had to be man because it was man who had sinned, and God could not punish any other creature as man's perfect sacrifice for sin. God's children, whom He wanted to redeem, were "flesh and blood." The sacrifice for their sins had to be the same:

> Inasmuch then as the children have partaken of flesh and blood, He Himself likewise shared in the same, that through death He might destroy him who had the power of death, that is, the devil…For indeed He does not give aid to angels, but He does give aid to the seed of Abraham [mankind].
> —HEBREWS 2:14, 16

We believe Jesus was human for the following reasons:

1. He had a human parent. He was born of a woman—the Virgin Mary (Matt. 1:18; John 2:1).

2. He had a human, physical nature of body, soul, and spirit. "The Word was made flesh" (John 1:14, KJV). "My soul is exceedingly sorrowful" (Matt. 26:38). "Father, 'into Your hands I commit My spirit'" (Luke 23:46).

3. He had human needs and emotions. "He [Jesus] was hungry" (Matt. 4:2). "Jesus…said, 'I thirst'" (John 19:28). "Jesus…being wearied with *his* journey" (John 4:6, KJV). "He was asleep" (Matt. 8:24). "Jesus wept" (John 11:35).

We also believe our Lord and Savior had to be God, because no mere man could carry the burden of God's wrath and satisfy His demands against sin. The apostle Peter states it in such a beautiful way: "You were not redeemed with corruptible things, like silver or gold, from your aimless conduct received by tradition from your fathers, but with the precious blood of Christ, as of a lamb without blemish and without spot" (1 Pet. 1:18–19).

JESUS: PROPHET, PRIEST, AND KING

This prophetic word is speaking of Jesus:

> The Spirit of the Lord God is upon Me, because the Lord has anointed Me to preach good tidings to the poor; He has sent Me to heal the brokenhearted, to proclaim liberty to the captives, and the opening of the prison to those who are bound.
>
> —ISAIAH 61:1

This prophecy is fulfilled in Luke 4:18–21, when Jesus came to Nazareth, His hometown.

We have already stated that Jesus was anointed by the Holy Spirit without measure. Some people in the Bible were anointed to be prophets, others to be priests, and still others to be kings. Jesus was anointed to be all of these: prophet, priest, and king.

1. He came as a *Prophet* to reveal God, to make known the very nature of God and also to speak the very Word of God:

The Lord your God will raise up for you a Prophet like me from your midst, from your brethren. Him you shall hear.

—DEUTERONOMY 18:15

God, who at various times and in various ways spoke in time past to the fathers by the prophets, has in these last days spoken to us by His Son, whom He has appointed heir of all things, through whom also He made the worlds.

—HEBREWS 1:1–2

2. He went to the cross, bearing the sins of the world, and became the *Priest* who offered the sacrifice to God:

For such a High Priest was fitting for us, who is holy, harmless, undefiled, separate from sinners, and has become higher than the heavens; who does not need daily, as those high priests, to offer up sacrifices, first for His own sins and then for the people's, for this He did once for all when He offered up Himself.

—HEBREWS 7:26–27

Not with the blood of goats and calves, but with His own blood He entered the Most Holy Place once for all, having obtained eternal redemption...how much more shall the blood of Christ, who through the eternal Spirit offered Himself without spot to God, cleanse your conscience from dead works to serve the living God?...not that He should offer Himself often, as the high priest enters the Most Holy Place every year with blood of another—He then would have had to suffer often since the foundation of the world; but now, once at the end of the ages, He has appeared to put away sin by the sacrifice of Himself.

—HEBREWS 9:12, 14, 25–26

3. Finally, He returned to sit on His throne as *King*. Jesus will not become king when He returns. He is now and has always been king; but the day will come when the whole world will acknowledge Him as King of kings and Lord of lords:

Rejoice greatly, O daughter of Zion! Shout, O daughter of Jerusalem! Behold, your King is coming to you; He is just and having salvation, lowly and riding on a donkey, a colt, the foal of a donkey.

—Zechariah 9:9

Who being the brightness of His glory and the express image of His person, and upholding all things by the word of His power, when He had by Himself purged our sins, sat down at the right hand of the Majesty on high.

—Hebrews 1:3

But we see Jesus, who was made a little lower than the angels, for the suffering of death crowned with glory and honor.

—Hebrews 2:9

Chapter 11

PART I
JESUS: HIS HUMILIATION
AND EXALTATION

IT SOUNDS STRANGE for us to use the word *humiliation* in relation to Jesus. Today, we see Him "high and lifted up," but it was not always so. Therefore, we must discuss the fact of His humiliation. What does it mean? What did it involve? Who made Him accept humiliation? We will answer all of these questions from the Word of God.

We have already made it clear that Jesus came to this earth as God and Man. He was omnipotent, all-powerful. No one had the power to force humiliation upon Him, so there is only one answer: He humbled Himself! While on earth, He humbled Himself to the limitations of man's flesh. He willingly refused to use His divine power to defend Himself. Instead, He presented Himself as a servant. He became sin for us that we might be delivered from sin.

Many theologians make this statement: Jesus did not give up His divine power at any time, but He willingly suspended the independent exercise of it. He always had the power, but He refused to use it. I believe this is true. Jesus explained it this way in Mark 10:45, "For even the Son of Man [note the human identity] did not come to be served, but to serve, and to give His life a ransom for many [paying the penalty for our sins]."

You will want to read and study the words in Philippians 2:5–11, but I would like to explain what happened—what Jesus did and what He did not do—in my own words. I believe in today's common English language, Paul would say it like this:

> Let your mind have the same opinion, or attitude, that Jesus manifested. He was God, but He did not demand His rights to be treated as God. Instead, He not only acted human, but He actually made Himself a servant. He humbled Himself to the extent He was willing to die on the cross like a common criminal. As a result, God exalted Him, giving Him a name that is above every other name. God has designed a glorious plan. At the name of Jesus, every knee is going to bow—whether in heaven, on earth, or under the earth—and every tongue [all mankind, all angelic powers, all demon powers, and even Satan] is going to confess that Jesus is the Christ, the Anointed One, and that He is Lord [God] to the glory of God the Father.

God's objective in all this is explained in Hebrews 2:14:

> Inasmuch then as the [earthly] children have partaken of flesh and blood, He Himself likewise shared in the same, that through death He might destroy him who had the power of death, that is, the devil.

We could write volumes on the subject of Christ's humiliation, but we will sum it up in these words. Jesus was conceived in the body of a woman (Luke 1:35) by the power of the Holy Spirit (Matt. 1:20). The prophets declared He would be born of a virgin in the little town of Bethlehem (Isa. 7:14, Mic. 5:2), and it happened just the way it was prophesied (Luke 2:4–5, 7).

The Suffering and Death of Jesus

The reason Jesus is able to understand us is that He was tempted in the same way we are tempted. He had human feelings and emotions. The writer of the Book of Hebrews explains this so clearly. He says Jesus is able to help us when we are tempted because He has gone through the same kind of suffering and temptation we experience. Jesus understands our weaknesses, having faced every human struggle, but He did not sin (Heb. 2:18, 4:15).

We must always understand that Jesus experienced all of this—the suffering, the persecution, the contempt—for us! Paul uses these grand words to describe it: "For you know the grace of our Lord Jesus Christ, that though He was rich, yet for your sakes He became poor, that you through His poverty might become rich" (2 Cor. 8:9).

The Bible teaches that God is a holy God. He will not tolerate sin. The people of Israel were told that God would not look upon them because of their sin (Isaiah 59:2). When Jesus was on the cross, He became sin for us so that we might become righteous in the sight of God. When that happened, when Jesus became sin (although He never committed sin), God the Father turned away from His Son. The writer of the first Gospel gave us these heartrending words in Matthew 27:46: "And about the ninth hour Jesus cried out with a loud voice, saying, 'Eli, Eli, lama sabachthani?' that is, 'My God, My God, why have You forsaken Me?'"

REDEMPTION AND RECONCILIATION

Before Jesus came, the world and all its people were in bondage to Satan because of sin. When Adam sinned, his sin passed to the whole human race. Paul tells us in Romans 3:10, 23: "There is none righteous, no, not one...for all have sinned and fall short of the glory of God." The coming of Jesus brought redemption. This word means "to buy back." We were slaves to sin, but Jesus paid the price, the penalty, and bought us with His own precious blood:

> In Him we have redemption through His blood, the forgiveness of sins, according to the riches of His grace.
>
> —EPHESIANS 1:7

> You were not redeemed with corruptible things, like silver or gold...but with the precious blood of Christ.
>
> —1 PETER 1:18–19

The Bible makes it clear that Jesus came to redeem us—to buy us back from death, from the power of sin, from Satan, and from the state of eternal separation from God:

> God was in Christ reconciling the world to Himself…and has committed to us the word of reconciliation. Now then, we are ambassadors for Christ, as though God were pleading through us; we implore you on Christ's behalf, be reconciled to God. For He made Him who knew no sin to be sin for us, that we might become the righteousness of God in Him.
>
> —2 CORINTHIANS 5:19–21

Jesus has not only redeemed us, but He has also reconciled us to God. This means we are restored to the divine favor of God, and our sins no longer separate us from Him. In fact, Jesus has delivered us from sin, from slavery to sin, and from eternal damnation:

> For as by one man's disobedience [Adam] many were made sinners, so also by one Man's obedience [Jesus] many will be made righteous.
>
> —ROMANS 5:19

> Who Himself bore our sins in His own body on the tree, that we, having died to sins, might live for righteousness—by whose stripes you were healed.
>
> —1 PETER 2:24

> Inasmuch then as the children have partaken of flesh and blood, He Himself likewise shared in the same, that through death He might destroy him who had the power of death, that is, the devil, and release those who through fear of death were all their lifetime subject to bondage.
>
> —HEBREWS 2:14–15

GOD'S ULTIMATE PLAN CONCERNING THE DEVIL

Through His death on the cross, Jesus conquered Satan. The devil no longer had the right to accuse us and condemn us. Through Christ we have power to overcome every work of the devil. The ultimate plan of

God is revealed in 1 John 3:8:

> He who sins is of the devil, for the devil has sinned from the beginning. For this purpose the Son of God was manifested [He appeared, showed Himself], that He might destroy the works of the devil.

Finally, in His act of redemption and reconciliation, Jesus became our substitute. The golden text of the Bible says, "God so loved the world that He gave His only begotten Son" (John 3:16). Speaking personally, He died in my place. He shed His blood to pay the penalty for my sin. This penalty for sin is death and eternal damnation, and Jesus paid it all for me:

> For He made Him who knew no sin to be sin for us, that we might become the righteousness of God in Him.
>
> —2 Corinthians 5:21

I am amazed as I consider the wonderful love of God—His marvelous plan of salvation, redemption, and reconciliation for the human race. The words of this great hymn seem to sum it up:[1]

> Oh, the love that drew salvation's plan!
> Oh, the grace that brought it down to man!
> Oh, the mighty gulf that God did span at Calvary!
> Mercy there was great, and grace was free;
> Pardon there was multiplied to me;
> There my burdened soul found liberty, at Calvary.
>
> —William R. Newell and Daniel B. Towner

PART II
THE EXALTATION OF CHRIST: WHAT DOES IT MEAN?

T HE WORDS *EXALT* and *exaltation* mean "to elevate above others, to lift up, to raise to the highest position." And just as certainly as Jesus suffered humiliation, He was also exalted by God the Father:

> Therefore God also has highly exalted Him and given Him the name which is above every name, that at the name of Jesus every knee should bow, of those in heaven, and of those on earth, and of those under the earth, and that every tongue should confess that Jesus Christ is Lord, to the glory of God the Father.
> —PHILIPPIANS 2:9–11

The exaltation of our Lord Jesus Christ deals with:

1. His Resurrection from the grave
2. The defeat of Satan
3. His ascension to the Father

4. The giving of ministry gifts to the church
5. His Second Coming back to the earth

THE RESURRECTION

The Bible teaches that Jesus stayed in the grave three days and three nights:

> For as Jonah was three days and three nights in the belly of the great fish, so will the Son of Man be three days and three nights in the heart of the earth.
>
> —MATTHEW 12:40

On the third day, Jesus came out of the grave, victorious over death, hell, sin, and the grave. The Bible gives abundant proof of this great event. First, we have the testimony of the apostles, who saw Him for forty days after His Resurrection:

> Him [Jesus] God raised up on the third day, and showed Him openly, not to all the people, but to witnesses chosen before by God, even to us who ate and drank with Him after He arose from the dead.
>
> —ACTS 10:40–41

> To whom [the apostles] He also presented Himself alive after His suffering by many infallible proofs, being seen by them during forty days and speaking of the things pertaining to the kingdom of God.
>
> —ACTS 1:3

The apostle Paul wraps it all up in this beautiful package in 1 Corinthians 15:3–8:

> For I delivered to you first of all that which I also received: [1] that Christ died for our sins according to the Scriptures, and [2] that He was buried, and [3] that He rose again the third day according to the Scriptures, and that [4] He was seen by Cephas [Peter], [5] then by the twelve. After that He was seen by [6] over five hundred brethren at once, of whom the greater part remain to the present,

but some have fallen asleep. After that [7] He was seen by James, then by all the apostles. Then last of all [8] He was seen by me also, as by one born out of due time.

The importance of the Resurrection

The importance of the Resurrection of Jesus cannot be overemphasized, and I must mention these two outstanding points:

1. The Resurrection of Jesus proves beyond any doubt that He was and is the Son of God:

[He is] declared to be the Son of God with power according to the Spirit of holiness, by the resurrection from the dead.

—ROMANS 1:4

2. His Resurrection proves that His promise of eternal life was not just an idle boast. We can depend on the promises of Jesus:

Jesus said to her [Martha], "I am the resurrection and the life. He who believes in Me, though he may die, he shall live. And whoever lives and believes in Me shall never die. Do you believe this?"

—JOHN 11:25–26

[Speaking to His disciples] A little while longer and the world will see Me no more, but you will see Me. Because I live, you will live also.

—JOHN 14:19

By His Resurrection, Jesus triumphed over every power of the devil:

[Jesus] disarmed principalities and powers, [and] He made a public spectacle of them, triumphing over them in it.

—COLOSSIANS 2:15

THE ASCENSION OF JESUS TO THE FATHER

Concerning His ascension into heaven, the Bible tells us that Jesus is our Forerunner. He is the One who shows the way and proves it can be done.

He not only ascended to the throne of God; He rules as the Head of the church:

> And if I go and prepare a place for you, I will come again and receive you to Myself; that where I am, there you may be also.
> —JOHN 14:3

> The working of His [God's] mighty power which He worked in Christ when He raised Him from the dead and seated Him at His right hand in the heavenly places, far above all principality and power and might and dominion, and every name that is named, not only in this age but also in that which is to come. And He put all things under His feet, and gave Him to be head over all things to the church, which is His body, the fullness of Him who fills all in all.
> —EPHESIANS 1:19–23

> The forerunner has entered for us, even Jesus, having become High Priest forever according to the order of Melchizedek.
> —HEBREWS 6:20

JESUS GAVE MINISTRY GIFTS TO HIS CHURCH

Later, we will study about the spiritual gifts the Holy Spirit gives us. We will also learn about the ministry gifts Jesus gave to the church. I call these "ascension gift ministries" because they were given when Jesus ascended, and they came into operation after the outpouring of the Holy Spirit on the Day of Pentecost:

> (He who descended is also the One who ascended far above all the heavens, that He might fill all things.) And He Himself gave some to be apostles, some prophets, some evangelists, and some pastors and teachers, for the equipping [perfecting] of the saints for the work of ministry, for the edifying of the body of Christ.
> —EPHESIANS 4:10–12

Jesus—Our Prophet, Priest and King

Jesus prophesied His death, burial, and Resurrection. He also promised to prepare a place for us and then return for us. Until He comes back to earth, He is seated "at the right hand of the Majesty on high," pleading our cause and making intercession for us (Heb. 1:3):

> The Lord [God] said to my Lord [Jesus], "Sit at My right hand, till I make Your enemies Your footstool."
>
> —Psalm 110:1

The fulfillment for this prophecy is in Matthew 22:44:

> It is Christ who died, and furthermore is also risen, who is even at the right hand of God, who also makes intercession for us.
>
> —Romans 8:34

> My little children, these things I write to you, so that you may not sin. And if anyone sins, we have an Advocate with the Father, Jesus Christ the righteous.
>
> —1 John 2:1

The Second Coming

Jesus is coming back! The Scriptures emphatically teach that He will return to earth, and put down all evil and rebellion. This subject is so vast that we cannot cover every detail, but here are the important points concerning His Second Coming:

- Jesus' Second Coming is not just a "spiritual appearing" but a visible, bodily appearing:

> [The angels spoke to Jesus' disciples] Men of Galilee, why do you stand gazing up into heaven? This same Jesus, who was taken up from you into heaven, will so come in like manner as you saw Him go into heaven.
>
> —Acts 1:11

Behold, He is coming with clouds, and every eye will see Him, even they who pierced Him. And all the tribes of the earth will mourn because of Him. Even so, Amen.

—REVELATION 1:7

- Jesus came the first time to die for the sins of the world. The next time, He will come as Judge. We do not know when this will be. In fact, the Bible tells us no one knows the day or the hour of His Second Coming:

But of that day and hour no one knows, not even the angels in heaven, nor the Son, but only the Father.

—MARK 13:32

He has appointed a day on which He will judge the world in righteousness by the Man [Jesus] whom He has ordained. He has given assurance of this to all by raising Him from the dead.

—ACTS 17:31

But the day of the Lord will come as a thief in the night, in which the heavens will pass away with a great noise, and the elements will melt with fervent heat; both the earth and the works that are in it will be burned up.

—2 PETER 3:10

And then the lawless one [the Antichrist] will be revealed, whom the Lord will consume with the breath of His mouth and destroy with the brightness of His coming.

—2 THESSALONIANS 2:8

When Jesus returns, everything will be put right. Satan will stand before the whole world as a defeated foe. All enemies of God will be destroyed. The most beautiful thing for the people of God is that their redemption, which is already complete in Jesus, will be demonstrated to the whole world:

Then comes the end, when He delivers the kingdom to God the Father, when He puts an end to all rule and all authority and power. For He must reign till He has put all enemies under His feet. The last enemy that will be destroyed is death.

—1 CORINTHIANS 15:24–26

[On the heavenly scene] And they sang a new song, saying: "You [Jesus] are worthy to take the scroll, and to open its seals; for You were slain, and have redeemed us to God by your blood out of every tribe and tongue and people and nation."

—REVELATION 5:9

Chapter 12

CHRIST INTRODUCES THE KINGDOM

O NE OF THE most exciting subjects in the Bible is the kingdom of God. The kingdom of God is the dominion of almighty God. It is both an authority (reign) and a place (realm). It involves the whole creation of God. It is the kingly rule of God over every person, place, and thing. We learn something of the magnitude of this kingdom from these words in the Psalm: "The Lord has established His throne in heaven, and His kingdom rules over all" (Ps. 103:19). This is an awesome statement. From His heavenly throne, God rules over everything He has made in His universe—in the heavens and on the earth.

Daniel, a great prophet in the Old Testament, gives us some insight on God's great kingdom. This man Daniel was a captive in the land of Nebuchadnezzar, the king of Babylon. The king had a very disturbing dream, and he asked all his wise men to tell him the dream and give him the interpretation or understanding of it. None was able to do this. Daniel was brought into the presence of the king, and he spoke these words to him:

You, O king, were watching; and behold, a great image! This great image, whose splendor was excellent, stood before you; and its form was awesome. This image's head was of fine gold, its chest and arms of silver, its belly and thighs of bronze, its legs of iron, its feet partly of iron and partly of clay. You watched while a stone was cut out without hands, which struck the image on its feet of iron and clay, and broke them in pieces. Then the iron, the clay, the bronze, the silver, and the gold were crushed together, and became like chaff from the summer threshing floors; the wind carried them away so that no trace of them was found. And the stone that struck the image became a great mountain and filled the whole earth.

—DANIEL 2:31–35

These are most unusual words, but the prophet did not stop at this point. God also gave him the interpretation of the dream:

1. Nebuchadnezzar, the ruler of Babylon, was the head of gold. This was the most powerful kingdom the world had ever known:

Wherever the children of men dwell, or the beasts of the field and the birds of the heaven, He has given them into your hand, and has made you ruler over them all—you are this head of gold.

—DANIEL 2:38

2. The next kingdom that would arise would be weaker than Babylon, but still very powerful. History remembers it as the kingdom of the Medes and Persians. This was the chest and arms of silver.

3. Then came the Hellenistic (Greek) Empire. This kingdom, the belly and thighs of bronze, was brought into existence by Alexander the Great, who conquered most of the known world by the time he was thirty-three years old. When Alexander, the "belly of bronze," died, his kingdom was divided into four parts, but only two of these divisions (the thighs) had significance.

4. The Roman Empire, the fourth kingdom, conquered the total Greek kingdom. Rome was ruling when the New Testament

began. It was symbolized by the legs of iron (the kingdom was ultimately divided into two parts, the eastern and western kingdoms). The Roman Empire was ruled by leaders called Caesars. In the beginning, this was a strong kingdom. However, over a period of time, it became weakened (the mixture of iron and clay). Daniel described the Roman Empire with these words:

And the fourth kingdom shall be as strong as iron, inasmuch as iron breaks in pieces and shatters everything; and like iron that crushes, that kingdom will break in pieces and crush all the others. Whereas you saw the feet and toes, partly of potter's clay and partly of iron, the kingdom shall be divided; yet the strength of the iron shall be in it, just as you saw the iron mixed with ceramic clay. And as the toes of the feet were partly of iron and partly of clay, so the kingdom shall be partly strong and partly fragile. As you saw iron mixed with ceramic clay, they will mingle with the seed of men; but they will not adhere to one another, just as iron does not mix with clay.

—DANIEL 2:40–43

THE STONE THAT CRUSHED ALL OTHER KINGDOMS

Then something happened that only God could know and reveal through His prophet Daniel. The Anointed One, the Messiah, came into the world in the form of one who was both God and Man—the Lord Jesus Christ. Virgin born, He was the "stone . . . cut out of the mountain without hands" (Dan. 2:45). In the days of the Caesars, God began to set up a kingdom that would never cease to exist and would never be destroyed:

And in the days of these kings [the Roman Caesars] the God of heaven will set up a kingdom which shall never be destroyed; and the kingdom shall not be left to other people; it shall break in pieces and consume all these kingdoms, and it shall stand forever. Inasmuch as you saw that the stone [Jesus, the Christ] was cut out of the mountain without hands [He came by the miracle of God the Father], and that it broke in pieces the iron, the bronze, the clay, the silver, and the gold—the great God has made known to the king what will come to pass after this. The dream is certain, and its interpretation is sure.

—DANIEL 2:44–45

The Roman Empire was the continuation and culmination of all the kingdoms that had gone before. When "the Stone" came rolling into the human race, God Himself had come to mankind. Through the life of Jesus—through His death, burial, resurrection, ascension, and the outpouring of the Holy Spirit—a kingdom was begun that would defeat the influence and the power of every other kingdom that had ever existed.

The great revelation of the New Testament is the church. The word *church* is first mentioned in the New Testament in this statement from Jesus: "On this rock I will build My church, and the gates [strength and influence] of Hades shall not prevail against it" (Matt. 16:18).

The victorious word about God's kingdom and about this church of the Lord Jesus is revealed in these words from the prophet Daniel:

> Then the kingdom and dominion, and the greatness of the kingdoms under the whole heaven, shall be given to the people, the saints of the Most High. His kingdom is an everlasting kingdom, and all dominions shall serve and obey Him.
>
> —Daniel 7:27

The Announcement of the Kingdom
in the New Testament

John the Baptist was the first herald (announcer) of the kingdom in the New Testament. He did not tell when the events of the kingdom would take place. He offered no timetable. His message was simple: "The kingdom of God is at hand"—God is getting ready to visit His people:

> In those days John the Baptist came preaching in the wilderness of Judea, and saying, "Repent, for the kingdom of heaven is at hand!"
>
> —Matthew 3:1–2

Jesus, like John the Baptist, began His earthly ministry preaching the kingdom of God. But there was an important difference between the ministry of John and Jesus. John did not know when the visitation of God in His kingdom would begin, but Jesus said, "The time is fulfilled"—it had already started:

> Now after John was put in prison, Jesus came to Galilee, preaching
> the gospel of the kingdom of God, and saying, "The time is fulfilled,
> and the kingdom of God is at hand. Repent and believe the gospel."
> —MARK 1:14–15

> And Jesus went about all Galilee, teaching in their synagogues,
> preaching the gospel of the kingdom, and healing all kinds of
> sickness and all kinds of disease among the people.
> —MATTHEW 4:23

Beyond any shadow of doubt, the Bible reveals Jesus to be the King over the kingdom of God. Remember, our basis of truth is the Bible, the Word of God. The following scriptures speak very plainly concerning the person of Jesus and His relationship to the kingdom:

> Now to [Jesus Christ] the King eternal, immortal, invisible, to God
> who alone is wise, be honor and glory forever and ever. Amen.
> —1 TIMOTHY 1:17

> I urge you in the sight of God who gives life to all things, and
> before Christ…He who is the blessed and only Potentate, the
> King of kings and Lord of lords.
> —1 TIMOTHY 6:13, 15

On His final week before going to the cross, Jesus came into Jerusalem and presented Himself to Israel in what we call the triumphant entry into Jerusalem. In doing this, Jesus was fulfilling Old Testament prophecy. In the Book of Zechariah the prophet, we find these words:

> Rejoice greatly, O daughter of Zion! Shout, O daughter of Jerusa-
> lem! Behold, your King is coming to you; He is just and having sal-
> vation, lowly and riding on a donkey, a colt, the foal of a donkey.
> —ZECHARIAH 9:9

This King was coming, and He would bring salvation! You can feel the drama as you see this prophecy come to pass:

> The next day a great multitude that had come to the feast, when
> they heard that Jesus was coming to Jerusalem, took branches of

palm trees and went out to meet Him, and cried out: "Hosanna! 'Blessed is He who comes in the name of the Lord!' The King of Israel!" Then Jesus, when He had found a young donkey, sat on it; as it is written: "Fear not, daughter of Zion; Behold, your King is coming, sitting on a donkey's colt."

—JOHN 12:12–15

The problem with every kingdom is its defense. The Babylonian kingdom became weak, and its leaders defied the God of heaven. The day came when the kingdom of the Medes and Persians defeated Babylon. Later, the Greeks came and defeated the Persian Empire. Then, the Romans rose up and defeated the Greeks. Finally we read about Jesus, the Stone cut out without hands, and through the ages we have watched as this Stone has crushed and overcome all the kingdoms of man.

Now, it is time for two important questions:

- What or who is the natural enemy of Jesus and the kingdom of God?

- Can God, can Jesus successfully defend this kingdom and cause it to be triumphant?

The first answer: the devil and his demons are the frontline enemies of God and His kingdom. We have already studied about Lucifer and his rebellion against God. As we read the New Testament, we see Satan and his demon powers doing all in their power to overcome and destroy Jesus.

The answer to the second question is a powerful yes! Jesus is more than enough. At every point in His earthly ministry, Jesus overcame Satan, his demon powers, and his kingdom.

The casting out of demon spirits is an important work in the ministry of Jesus, and it is very necessary that the church continues in this ministry and demonstrates this power. When demons are in control, they work against God's authority. The ability to cast out demons demonstrates the power and presence of the kingdom of God over every satanic force—over all the works of the devil. The Bible tells us Jesus was manifested (revealed, came on the scene) that He might destroy the works of the devil. (See 1 John 3:8.) Jesus Himself testified that when He was casting out demons, He was doing the work of the kingdom of God:

> But if I with the finger of God cast out devils [demons], no doubt
> the kingdom of God is come upon you. When a strong man armed
> keepeth his palace, his goods are in peace: but when a stronger
> than he shall come upon him, and overcome him, he taketh from
> him all his armour wherein he trusted, and divideth his spoils.
> —LUKE 11:20–22, KJV

Satan is the "strong man" who tries to keep God's people in bondage;
but when the "stronger than he" (this stronger One is Jesus) comes against
the devil, guess who wins!

THREE KINGDOM-CENTERED AREAS IN THE LIFE OF JESUS

As we watch Jesus operate, as we hear His words, it is obvious He is greatly
concerned about this kingdom message. This is illustrated by three facets
of His earthly ministry:

1. The Sermon on the Mount is the greatest message Jesus gave
   while He was on earth. This sermon is a series of messages or
   statements Jesus taught His disciples. The purpose of the statements was to declare to the people the laws of the kingdom
   of God. The Sermon on the Mount is to the New Testament
   [covenant] what the Ten Commandments and the Law are to
   the Old Testament [covenant]. Matthew uses the word *kingdom*
   eight times as he records the words of Jesus in this sermon.

2. The parables of Jesus were told to illustrate the kingdom. These
   parables are earthly stories with heavenly (spiritual) meaning.
   Almost all the parables of Jesus were told to reveal some truth
   about the kingdom of God. Here are two examples:

> Another parable He put forth to them, saying: "The kingdom of
> heaven is like a mustard seed."
> —MATTHEW 13:31

> Then He said, "To what shall we liken the kingdom of God? Or
> with what parable shall we picture it? It is like a mustard seed."
> —MARK 4:30–31

117

These scriptures begin the same parable, recorded by both Matthew and Mark. Notice, the phrases *kingdom of heaven* and *kingdom of God* are used interchangeably.

> 3. The miracles of Jesus are important in the study of the kingdom of God. His miracles show the nature of His kingdom. By His miracles, Jesus revealed His power over nature, demonstrated His ability to supply the needs of mankind, and openly defeated Satan's kingdom! Jesus issued this challenge to any who doubted His power and authority:

> If I do not do the works of My Father, do not believe Me; but if I do, though you do not believe Me, believe the works, that you may know and believe that the Father is in Me, and I in Him.
> —John 10:37–38

Here is a good project for your Bible study time. Read the dramatic stories of the following miracles. They all demonstrate Christ's kingdom power in many exciting ways:

- Jesus changes the water into wine. See John 2:1–11.

- Jesus stills the storm. See Matt. 8:23–27; Mark 4:35–41; and Luke 8:22–25.

- The feeding of the five thousand (the only miracle told in all four Gospels). See Matt. 14:15–21; Mark 6:34–44; Luke 9:12–17; and John 6:5–14.

- Jesus walking on the water. See Matt. 14:22–33; Mark 6:45–52; and John 6:15–21.

As we close this chapter, I want to clarify one point. Many teachers use complicated methods to prove a difference between the kingdom of heaven and the kingdom of God. I do not believe this teaching is valid. There has always been and will always be only one kingdom of a godly nature—the kingdom of the God of heaven.

Chapter 13

WOUNDED, BRUISED, CHASTISED, AND HEALED

IN THE OLD Testament, the greatest prophetic revelation of Jesus Christ and His earthly ministry is given to us by the prophet Isaiah. The central theme of our lesson is found in the Book of Isaiah, chapter 53:

> Who has believed our report? And to whom has the arm of the Lord been revealed? For He shall grow up before Him as a tender plant, and as a root out of dry ground. He has no form or comeliness [His looks would not have attracted our attention]; and when we see Him, there is no beauty that we should desire Him. He is despised and rejected by men, a Man of sorrows and acquainted with grief. And we hid, as it were, our faces from Him; He was despised, and we did not esteem Him [we were not interested; we did not care about Him nor honor Him]. Surely He has borne our griefs and carried our sorrows; yet we esteemed Him stricken, smitten by God, and afflicted [we felt all His problems were punishment from God]. But He was wounded for our transgressions, He was bruised for our

iniquities; the chastisement for our peace was upon Him, and by His stripes we are healed. All we like sheep have gone astray; we have turned, every one, to his own way; and the Lord has laid on Him the iniquity of us all.

—Isaiah 53:1–6

The Hebrew word for "esteem" and "esteemed" is *chashab*. It is a "huge" word, with the idea that we "fabricated a mental idea regarding His value, that we did not honor Him—and we felt what He was getting, He deserved."

These are powerful words, and it is true that God sent His own Son Jesus to do great and miraculous things for us. But we have some questions to consider: Why did He do it? Why was it necessary? The first question has an easy Bible answer: "For God so loved the world that He gave His only begotten Son" (John 3:16). It is so simple it seems unbelievable, but it is true. God loves the sinful world—and us!

Now, why was it necessary? Let's go back to the garden. As the result of Adam's sin and transgression, we were in bondage to Satan. Jesus became a Man and took our sins, our sorrow, our iniquities, and our diseases upon Himself. The wrath of God had come upon the human race, and now Jesus paid the total penalty for all our transgressions. To deliver us from Satan's bondage, He paid the ransom—our total debt—so we could go free. He identified with our sin, our iniquities, and our sicknesses, bringing us to a place of peace with God.

When Jesus came, God, in the form of man, not only became our Savior, but also our Servant. Jesus clearly confessed His servant role. Paul declared it as well. Jesus taught this principle of servant ministry to His disciples and gave them this advice:

You know that the rulers of the Gentiles lord it over them, and those who are great exercise authority over them. Yet it shall not be so among you; but whoever desires to become great among you, let him be your servant. And whoever desires to be first among you, let him be your slave—just as the Son of Man did not come to be served, but to serve, and to give His life a ransom for many.

—Matthew 20:25–28

The words of Paul are very descriptive:

> [He] made Himself of no reputation, taking the form of a bond-servant, and coming in the likeness of men. And being found in appearance as a man, He humbled Himself and became obedient to the point of death, even the death of the cross.
>
> —PHILIPPIANS 2:7–8

When Jesus died on the cross, He fulfilled the words of the prophet Isaiah. At Calvary, He purchased wonderful benefits for us. Four major benefits are listed in Isaiah 53.

HE WAS WOUNDED FOR OUR TRANSGRESSIONS

The law of God demanded sacrifice—the shedding of blood—to pay the penalty for the sins of mankind. Jesus became that sacrifice. He took our place before God. He became sin for us and took the punishment for our sins:

> Christ has redeemed us from the curse of the law, having become a curse for us (for it is written, "Cursed is everyone who hangs on a tree").
>
> —GALATIANS 3:13

> For He made Him who knew no sin to be sin for us, that we might become the righteousness of God in Him.
>
> —2 CORINTHIANS 5:21

Through Jesus, we now have the forgiveness of sins and eternal life. Forgiveness does not come to us because we deserve it or earn it by good works. Forgiveness is ours when we confess our sins to God, turn from them (the Bible calls this repentance), and ask for His forgiveness. At that moment, our soul is cleansed by the blood of Jesus Christ and we receive eternal life:

> In Him we have redemption through His blood, the forgiveness of sins, according to the riches of His grace.
>
> —EPHESIANS 1:7

Jesus said, "He who hears My word and believes in Him who sent Me has everlasting life, and shall not come into judgment, but has passed from death into life" (John 5:24).

The devil does not want us to believe the Word of God. He does not want us to believe our sins are forgiven and that we now belong to God. But we must believe God's Word, for it is not only a source of information, but it is the source of life:

> These things I have written to you who believe in the name of the Son of God, that you may know that you have eternal life, and that you may continue to believe in the name of the Son of God.
>
> —1 John 5:13

When we believe God's Word, confess our sin and turn from it, and stand on the promises of God's Word, we can be assured our sins are forgiven:

> If we confess our sins, He is faithful and just to forgive us our sins and to cleanse us from all unrighteousness.
>
> —1 John 1:9

He Was Bruised for Our Iniquities

The second benefit mentioned in Isaiah 53 deals with the subject of iniquity. This iniquity is a natural part of our life. Sin is the actual transgression, the breaking of the law. Iniquity is the natural power of evil that works in us when we are without God. In our natural state, we all have a tendency toward certain sins and weaknesses:

> We all once conducted ourselves in the lusts of our flesh, fulfilling the desires of the flesh and of the mind, and were by nature children of wrath, just as the others.
>
> —Ephesians 2:3

These iniquities—traits and habits—are passed down from generation to generation. Many young men and women look at the weaknesses and sinful practices of their parents and grandparents and say, "What's the use?" But, through Jesus and the power of His cross, we can break the curse of past generations and put our foot on every habit and bondage in our own personal life.

When we speak of the fact that Jesus was bruised for our iniquities, we mean that our iniquities became His; He suffered on our behalf:

> All we like sheep have gone astray; we have turned, every one, to his own way; and the Lord has laid on Him the iniquity of us all.
> —ISAIAH 53:6

In the Bible, the presence of sinful habits and traits passed to us through Adam and all of our ancestors is sometimes called "the old man" and "the body of sin." We do not have to serve this "old man" any more. We do not have to serve the power of lust, greed, hate, jealousy, or any other sinful practice:

> Our old man was crucified with Him, that the body of sin might be done away with, that we should no longer be slaves of sin.
> —ROMANS 6:6

Let us understand that our children will not automatically be born again and inherit eternal life. Every person must come before God in true repentance and faith to receive salvation. There is, however, a great advantage. Our children and grandchildren will have godly parents and grandparents who set the right example before them, with a tendency toward righteousness and not the tendency toward evil.

HE WAS CHASTISED FOR OUR PEACE

The third benefit listed in Isaiah 53 deals with the subject of peace. Through the work of Jesus Christ on the cross, we can have peace of mind and emotions. We can live in peace with those around us, but most important we can have peace with God. This peace gives us freedom from fear and anxiety, bringing us into harmony with God Himself:

> And, having made peace through the blood of his cross, by him to reconcile all things unto himself; by him, I say, whether they be things in earth, or things in heaven.
> —COLOSSIANS 1:20, KJV

An important fact to remember is this: We have peace with God because we are now reconciled to God. Also, through the presentation of the gospel, we act on the authority of Jesus Christ and can reconcile others to God:

> Now all things are of God, who has reconciled us to Himself through Jesus Christ, and has given us the ministry of reconciliation.
>
> —2 Corinthians 5:18

It is a simple thing to find this peace of God and have peace with God, but there are some pitfalls along the way. Many people insist on going in the wrong direction. Some people look for peace by going to a so-called professional counselor. Many times they are told to dig up all the hurts and garbage of the past so they can examine it, deal with it, and thereby get over it. This is not the path of deliverance. Paul the Apostle tells us to forget those things that are behind (Phil. 3:13). By constantly digging into our past memories, we magnify the problems.

If someone has wounded us, we must confront the person and the problem, settle it, forgive and forget, and then move on to victory in Jesus! Many people look for peace by using drugs and alcohol, legally and illegally. They receive some temporary relief, but soon they are using larger and larger doses to maintain a state of tranquility. Often this "cure" is worse than the original problem, and they end up emotionally, spiritually, and in reality—dead!

The simple way—the only successful way to find peace—is to come to God for help. When we call on the Lord, confessing our sin and asking for His forgiveness, we receive His salvation and peace with God. We are justified, meaning that we become righteous in the sight of God. We are completely cleansed from all sin, and it is "just as if we had never sinned." We are delivered from all guilt and condemnation:

> Therefore, having been justified by faith, we have peace with God through our Lord Jesus Christ.
>
> —Romans 5:1

> There is therefore now no condemnation to those who are in Christ Jesus, who do not walk according to the flesh, but according to the Spirit.
>
> —Romans 8:1

For God has not given us a spirit of fear, but of power and of love and of a sound mind.

—2 TIMOTHY 1:7

We cannot leave this subject without raising a flag of caution. In order to have this peace working in us, we must deal with forgiveness. It is impossible to walk in godly peace while we hold others in the bondage of unforgiveness. The words of Jesus on this subject are powerful:

For if you forgive men their trespasses, your heavenly Father will also forgive you. But if you do not forgive men their trespasses, neither will your Father forgive your trespasses.

—MATTHEW 6:14–15

The most beautiful part of peace with God is that it can be a permanent part of our lives. Here is the formula for maintaining this peace:

- If we will direct our thoughts toward God and not toward sinful fantasies;

- If we stay in the Bible, the Word of God, and walk in obedience to it;

- We can then keep our faith strong, and this peace will abide (remain, live) with us:

You [God] will keep him in perfect peace, whose mind is stayed on You, because he trusts in You.

—ISAIAH 26:3

Jesus left this promise with His disciples. It is good advice for us:

Peace I leave with you, My peace I give to you; not as the world gives do I give to you. Let not your heart be troubled, neither let it be afraid.

—JOHN 14:27

WE ARE HEALED BY HIS STRIPES

The fourth benefit mentioned in Isaiah 53 deals with healing. It is amazing that so many wonderful things happen to us because Jesus was willing to suffer and die for us. Isaiah 53:5 declares, "By His stripes we are healed." When we read the four Gospels, we see Jesus healing the sick. When He sends His disciples out to preach the gospel, He also commissions them to heal the sick. It is easy to see that this healing power was a great part of His earthly ministry. The stripes that were placed upon Him can bring us healing of every kind—physically, spiritually, and emotionally. In the Gospels, we see Jesus not only healing the sick, but we learn why He healed them. He was not only loving them, but He was fulfilling prophecy:

> When evening had come, they brought to Him many who were demon-possessed. And He cast out the spirits with a word, and healed all who were sick, that it might be fulfilled which was spoken by Isaiah the prophet, saying: "He Himself took our infirmities and bore our sicknesses."
>
> —MATTHEW 8:16–17

> Who Himself bore our sins in His own body on the tree, that we, having died to sins, might live for righteousness—by whose stripes you were healed.
>
> —1 PETER 2:24

Sin, sickness, suffering, death. Where did it all begin? Why would a God of love allow sickness to be a part of our lives? Many doubters ask these questions and turn away as if there were no answer. But there is an answer, and once again, it begins in the garden.

I want to make two statements, and I will prove them by the Word of God:

1. All sin, sickness, suffering, and death began with one man.

2. All help, all healing, all deliverance comes to us by the work of one Man:

> Through one man [Adam] sin entered the world, and death
> through sin, and thus death spread to all men, because all sinned.
>
> —ROMANS 5:12

> For since by man [Adam] came death, by Man [Jesus] also came
> the resurrection of the dead. For as in Adam all die, even so in
> Christ all shall be made alive.
>
> —1 CORINTHIANS 15:21–22

Without Adam's transgression, there would be no sickness; without Jesus, there would be no hope or healing. This idea is expressed beautifully in these words of Jesus in John 10:10: "The thief does not come except to steal, and to kill, and to destroy. I have come that they may have life, and that they may have it more abundantly." The question must be asked: If Jesus came to bring healing, why are sickness and disease still present in the world?

God spoke through an Old Testament prophet, saying, "My people are destroyed for lack of knowledge" (Hosea 4:6). Sickness is in the world today for the same reason that sin is still with us: people do not realize what Jesus has purchased for them. We must "know our rights." We must exercise faith. We must stand on the Word of God. The work and ministry of healing can be complicated if we listen to the words of unbelief from the "natural man." So, let us make some pointed, declarative statements, and then let us prove these statements with the Word of God.

God wants us to prosper and be in good health.

This prosperity is in the physical, the spiritual, the financial, and the emotional. It applies to every facet of our life:

> Beloved, I pray that you may prosper in all things and be in health,
> just as your soul prospers [that your body will be as healthy as
> your soul].
>
> —3 JOHN 2

The road to healing begins with proper believing and proper confessing of God's Word.

> For with the heart one believes unto righteousness, and with the
> mouth confession is made unto salvation.
>
> —ROMANS 10:10

Salvation is the Greek word *soteria*, pronounced "so-tay-ree'-ah." It means "deliverance, physically and spiritually."

Healing comes to us through faith in God's Word. This is revealed in the ministry of Jesus.

> And suddenly, a woman who had a flow of blood for twelve years came from behind and touched the hem of His garment...But Jesus turned around, and when He saw her He said, "Be of good cheer, daughter; your faith has made you well." And the woman was made well from that hour.
>
> —MATTHEW 9:20, 22

> And when He had come into the house, the blind men came to Him. And Jesus said to them, "Do you believe that I am able to do this?" They said to Him, "Yes, Lord."
>
> —MATTHEW 9:28–29

Unbelief can hinder us from receiving our healing. Jesus needs a "faith response."

In the area where He grew up, He did not get this response of faith:

> Now He could do no mighty work there, except that He laid His hands on a few sick people and healed them. And He marveled because of their unbelief.
>
> —MARK 6:5–6

Other things can hinder the healing work. If we do not deal with sin and iniquity in our lives, we separate ourselves from God's mercy (Ps. 66:18; Isa. 59:2). If we come to the Lord's table—Communion—in an unworthy manner, we bring damnation and judgment upon ourselves (1 Cor. 11:29).

We can receive healing in many different ways:

1. By personal prayer (James 5:16).

2. By calling for the elders of the church (James 5:14–15).

3. By the laying on of hands (Mark 16:17–18).

4. By the creative word of faith (Ps. 107:20).

5. The proper observance of the Lord's Supper. When we receive Communion, we "proclaim the Lord's death," and we can receive everything He purchased for us on the cross (1 Cor. 11:23–26).

6. During the time of praise and worship in the church, great power is manifested. This is the time to move in and receive (Ps. 8:2, 32:7; Matt. 21:16).

When we truly turn our lives over to God, we will become obedient to His Word. In order to become obedient, we must repent (turn from our way to God's way), have faith in God for the forgiveness of our sins, and be water baptized.

Chapter 14

Repentance, Faith, and Water Baptism

Part I: Repentance

M ANY PEOPLE HAVE different ideas about the word *repentance*, but it is a simple word. It begins with an anxiety arising from the awareness of guilt or need in our life. Some people have this awareness and become sorry for their lifestyle of sin, but they stop there. This is not repentance. We can be sorry for our sin but never truly repent. In true repentance, there must be a change of mind, attitude, and direction that will cause us to turn from our way to God's way. This turning will lead to a transformation of our lifestyle—our attitudes and activities.

We must understand one important thing before we go into this study: we do not decide to repent. Repentance, this ability to turn, is a gift from God. We can say yes or no to God's prompting, but the initiative comes from Him. When the Gentiles heard the gospel from Peter, they believed his word and received God's salvation. This was a great surprise to the Jewish believers in Jerusalem; nevertheless, "they glorified God, saying, 'Then God has also granted to the Gentiles repentance to life'" (Acts 11:18). Peter, speaking to Jewish leaders about Jesus, made this statement:

"Him God has exalted to His right hand to be Prince and Savior, to give repentance to Israel and forgiveness of sins" (Acts 5:31).

We are born with a sinful nature, and the human desire is to enter into sinful paths. Once we repent and turn to God, everything is different. We no longer follow our way of sinful activity, but we go God's way of righteousness and live in obedience to His Word:

> Behold, I was brought forth in iniquity, and in sin my mother conceived me.
>
> —Psalm 51:5

> The carnal mind is enmity against God; for it is not subject to the law of God, nor indeed can be.
>
> —Romans 8:7, author's emphasis

> Put off, concerning your former conduct, the old man [the sinful nature] which grows corrupt according to the deceitful lusts.
>
> —Ephesians 4:22

What About This Thing Called "Sin"?

The word *sin* is described in the Old Testament as a "fault" or an "offense" against God. In the New Testament, the Greek word *hamartia* is used for sin. It too means an "offense," but it also has the idea of "missing the mark." When an individual shoots an arrow at the target, the idea is to hit the absolute center—the bull's-eye. When the arrow misses the center of perfection, the spotter cries out, "Hamartia!" He is saying, "You missed the mark!"

When we fail to live up to God's absolute standards, when we break the law of God and rebel against His Word, this is sin. In fact, every act of rebellion against the will of God is sin.

The following words give us an excellent understanding of what sin is:

> For out of the heart proceed evil thoughts, murders, adulteries, fornications, thefts, false witness, blasphemies.
>
> —Matthew 15:19

> When desire has conceived, it gives birth to sin; and sin, when it is full-grown, brings forth death.
>
> —James 1:15

131

> Therefore, to him who knows to do good and does not do it, to him it is sin.
>
> —JAMES 4:17

The writer James tells us it is not only sin to do what is wrong, but it is also sin to neglect what we know to be good. One big question: How do we find out what is right and what is wrong? Fortunately, when we want to learn this, we have a standard, an absolute. We have the Bible, the Word of God. King David had a lot of problems, but he knew the value of God's Word. In Psalm 119:11, he said to God, "Your word I have hidden in my heart, that I might not sin against You." In every question of life, in every problem we face, God's Word has the answer.

When we read about sin and realize we have sinned, we have only one intelligent response: How do we receive forgiveness for our sins, and how do we deal with the whole sin question? Our Bible has the answers: we must confess our sins to God and then forsake them, turning to His direction for our lives.

> If we confess our sins, He is faithful and just to forgive us our sins and to cleanse us from all unrighteousness.
>
> —1 JOHN 1:9

> And the tax collector, standing afar off, would not so much as raise his eyes to heaven, but beat his breast, saying, "God, be merciful to me a sinner!"
>
> —LUKE 18:13

> Let the wicked forsake his way, and the unrighteous man his thoughts; let him return to the Lord, and He will have mercy on him; and to our God, for He will abundantly pardon.
>
> —ISAIAH 55:7

One of the great blessings of our life is to learn that God is a good God! It is His goodness that causes us to repent and turn our lives over to Him.

> Do you despise the riches of His goodness, forbearance, and longsuffering, not knowing that the goodness of God leads you to repentance?
>
> —ROMANS 2:4

Finally, keep in mind that this repentance is not merely a casual teaching of theology. It is our starting place with God. The Bible teaches that we, by our good works, cannot deserve repentance, salvation, or anything from God. In fact, true repentance is "repentance from dead works." We must abandon all ideas that we deserve God's blessings. We must depend on God's grace, His goodness, and His mercy:

> Therefore leaving the principles [the beginning, the rule] of the doctrine [Word] of Christ, let us go on unto perfection [the completion, consummation, maturity]; not laying again the foundation of repentance from dead [same meaning as a corpse] works, and of faith toward God.
>
> —HEBREWS 6:1, KJV

PART II: FAITH TOWARD GOD

Faith is simply knowing and believing that God will do what He has promised in His Word. The classic definition of faith is in Hebrews 11:1:

> Now faith is the substance [the assurance and confidence] of things hoped for, the evidence [proof, seeing it before it happens] of things not seen.

Faith is also a part of the "doctrine of Christ" set forth in Hebrews 6:1. It is not simply called "faith," but "faith toward God." Through the ages, people have had many different attitudes toward God.

- Adam had rebellion toward God and believed Satan's words.

- Israel often had distrust toward God and rejected its true leaders and turned to idols.

- David was a wonderful example of faith toward God. Whatever God said, he believed and thereby reaped a rich reward in his life.

When we truly repent and turn to God in faith, we are brought into relationship with God. This is called justification, and it comes when our repentance works in harmony with our God-given faith. We must believe

Jesus died to pay the penalty for our sin. When I teach on this subject, I like to give two definitions of justification:

1. The theological definition: justification is the sovereign act of God whereby the believing sinner is declared (by God) to be righteous.

2. The simple but profound definition: "just-as-if-I-had-never-sinned":

For all have sinned and fall short of the glory of God, being justified freely by His grace through the redemption that is in Christ Jesus.

—ROMANS 3:23–24

Therefore, having been justified by faith, we have peace with God through our Lord Jesus Christ, through whom also we have access by faith into this grace in which we stand, and rejoice in hope of the glory of God.

—ROMANS 5:1–2

For He made Him who knew no sin to be sin for us, that we might become the righteousness of God in Him.

—2 CORINTHIANS 5:21

To make certain we understand how justification is obtained, we will let the Word explain.

- It starts when the Holy Spirit produces in us a godly sorrow about our sins:

For godly sorrow produces repentance leading to salvation.

—2 CORINTHIANS 7:10

- Because we have a carnal mind that is opposed to God (Rom. 8:7), the Holy Spirit must also impart a work of faith in us to believe the Word of God. Faith is the absolute, essential ingredient in our justification, our salvation:

Most assuredly, I say to you, he who hears My word and believes in Him who sent Me has everlasting life, and shall not come into judgment, but has passed from death into life.

—JOHN 5:24

If you confess with your mouth the Lord Jesus and believe in your heart that God has raised Him from the dead, you will be saved. For with the heart one believes unto righteousness, and with the mouth confession is made unto salvation.

—ROMANS 10:9–10

- We say faith is the essential ingredient in our salvation, but it is also essential in every part of our lives. We cannot do business with God without faith:

But without faith it is impossible to please Him, for he who comes to God must believe that He is, and that He is a rewarder of those who diligently seek Him.

—HEBREWS 11:6

Here is the great news about faith: everybody can have it! We receive faith when we hear God's Word, the Bible, being taught, preached, and prophesied. I highly recommend that we not only read the Bible, but that we often read it aloud. There is power in the written Word and the spoken Word.

WHAT ABOUT THIS "WORD" OF GOD?

In the New Testament, we have the word *logos*, which means "something said (including the thought), the expression of what an object actually is, a communication of an idea or doctrine." We refer to the Bible as "The Word (Logos) of God." In the Gospel of John, Jesus is called Logos—the living manifestation of God and His Word:

In the beginning was the Word [Logos], and the Word [Logos] was with God, and the Word [Logos] was God...And the Word [Logos] became flesh and dwelt among us.

—JOHN 1:1, 14

We also have the Greek word *rhema*, which means "an utterance, a specific topic or command." Rhema is used for a certain, definite occasion, involving a specific word to a specific person or situation. In Romans 10:17, we read, "So then faith comes by hearing, and hearing by the word [rhema—an utterance on a specific topic] of God."

We should read God's Word (Logos, the Bible), and while we read it we should expect to hear a specific word (rhema) of instruction that will produce great faith for our lives and our situations. People of great faith did not get that faith from a casual brush with God and His Word.

Part III: Water Baptism

Water baptism is a subject of much debate, so I want to be careful with my words. We often contest a teaching on the basis of personal prejudice and sometimes, religious tradition. I urge you not to make this mistake. Let's see what the Word of God has to say.

A great deal of biblical teaching on this subject is summed up in these two scriptures:

> What shall we say then? Shall we continue in sin that grace may abound? Certainly not! How shall we who died to sin live any longer in it? Or do you not know that as many of us as were baptized into Christ Jesus were baptized into His death? Therefore we were buried with Him through baptism into death, that just as Christ was raised from the dead by the glory of the Father, even so we also should walk in newness of life.
>
> —Romans 6:1–4

> For in Him dwells all the fullness of the Godhead bodily; and you are complete in Him, who is the head of all principality and power. In Him you were also circumcised with the circumcision made without hands, by putting off the body of the sins of the flesh, by the circumcision of Christ, [when you were] buried with Him in baptism, in which you also were raised with Him through faith in the working of God, who raised Him from the dead.
>
> —Colossians 2:9–12

First, let me make a simple, common sense statement: water baptism is either an empty form that should be discarded, or it is an essential experience (for full obedience) in the kingdom of God. If water baptism were only the "outward sign of an inward work," an empty ritual or mechanical form, then it would be useless. When Jesus died on the cross, He fulfilled the Law and satisfied the demands of God in relation to the sacrifice for sin. He destroyed all imagery and took the condemnation regarding holy days, new moon observances, and sabbaths and nailed them to His cross (Col. 2:14–17). They were finished. Surely there is no room in the teaching of the New Testament for a meaningless act of water baptism.

Yet after Jesus had fulfilled the Law in all points, after He died on the cross, after He was resurrected from the dead and ascended to the right hand of the Majesty on high, Peter, on the Day of Pentecost, instructed the people to "Repent, and be baptized" (Acts 2:38, KJV).

With these facts in mind, we will ask this important question: What is water baptism? I shall give a four-part answer to this question.

1. It is a burial.
2. It is the New Testament sign of covenant relationship.
3. It is the new covenant circumcision of heart.
4. It is a vital experience for repentant believers.

Baptism is a burial.

The pivot point for the believer and the Christian faith is identification. We first identify by faith. We then identify in water baptism. We continue to identify in our lifestyle of an obedient walk with Jesus.

- We can believe we are sinners and still be lost.

- We can believe Jesus died for our sins and still not have eternal life.

- A believing sinner must, in faith, identify with the death, burial, and resurrection of our Lord Jesus Christ.

This is done by faith in water baptism. Some say that "faith alone" is all that is necessary, but the Bible knows nothing of faith without obedience. True faith is never alone. It is always accompanied by obedience to the Word of God. The thief on the cross not only had faith to believe Jesus could help him, but he also called out to Him, thus identifying with Jesus rather than his own past lifestyle.

In our identification with Jesus, we must remember He was wholly buried, not just sprinkled or poured upon with dirt or stone. The Greek word for baptize is "baptizo." The true meaning of this word is "to make whelmed, fully wet."

Many groups have a tradition of sprinkling or pouring water upon an individual who comes for baptism, but Jesus warned the people that they were "making the word of God of none effect" through their traditions (Mark 7:13, KJV). Let's look at some Bible examples that clearly define these words related to baptism:

1. The story of Lazarus and the rich man:

Then he cried and said, "Father Abraham, have mercy on me, and send Lazarus that he may *dip* the tip of his finger in water and cool my tongue; for I am tormented in this flame."
—LUKE 16:24, AUTHOR'S EMPHASIS

2. At the Last Supper, the disciples asked who would betray Jesus:

Jesus answered, "It is he to whom I shall give a piece of bread when I have dipped it." And having *dipped* the bread, He gave it to Judas Iscariot, the son of Simon.
—JOHN 13:26, AUTHOR'S EMPHASIS

3. The Book of Revelation describes the Lord Jesus Christ with these words:

He was clothed with a robe *dipped* in blood, and His name is called The Word of God.
—REVELATION 19:13, AUTHOR'S EMPHASIS

In all these examples, when the words *dip* and *dipped* are used, it is "bapto," the foundational Greek root word for baptize and baptism. It is a verb, meaning "to whelm, that is, cover wholly with a fluid." The meaning is clear. New Testament baptism is by immersion.

Baptism is the New Testament sign of covenant relationship.

When God called Abraham and entered into covenant with him, He commanded him to respond with the sign of covenant obedience—circumcision:

> And God said to Abraham: "As for you, you shall keep My covenant, you and your descendants after you throughout their generations. This is My covenant which you shall keep, between Me and you and your descendants after you: every male child among you shall be circumcised; and you shall be circumcised in the flesh of your foreskins, and it shall be a sign of the covenant between Me and you."
>
> —GENESIS 17:9–11

Although this was a physical act that signified obedience to God's command, Abraham's descendants—the people of Israel—often failed God. They went so far as to worship idols like the heathen. What they really needed was a work in their heart, in the inner person. Before Moses left them, he gave them this important word:

> And the Lord your God will circumcise your heart and the heart of your descendants, to love the Lord your God with all your heart and with all your soul, that you may live.
>
> —DEUTERONOMY 30:6

In water baptism, by faith and obedience to the Word of God and most importantly by the operation of the Holy Spirit, the old man of sin is buried. There will be times of struggle and failure, but if there has been a true work of faith in repentance and water baptism, that old nature will not rule over you. We will come forth with the power to love the Lord our God with all our heart and with all our soul.

What shall we do when temptation or struggle comes? The Bible has the answer.

We are to "reckon" ourselves dead to sin and alive to God (Rom. 6:11). Many give up at the first sign of temptation and get it all wrong. They reckon themselves dead to God and alive to sin. According to our faith, what we believe and practice is what we get. We can have either defeat or victory!

Water baptism is the new covenant circumcision of heart for the believer.

As the circumcision of the Old Testament was an operation, so water baptism is in the New Testament. The operation is (1) by faith, (2) as we act in obedience to the Word of God, and (3) it is performed by the power of the Holy Spirit. We quoted earlier from Colossians 2, and the Amplified Version gives clear understanding of this:

> In Him also you were circumcised with a circumcision not made with hands, but in a [spiritual] circumcision [performed by] Christ by stripping off the body of the flesh (the whole corrupt, carnal nature with its passions and lusts). [Thus you were circumcised when] you were buried with Him in [your] baptism, in which you were also raised with Him [to a new life] through [your] faith in the working of God [as displayed] when He raised Him up from the dead.
>
> —COLOSSIANS 2:11–12, AMP

Remember, those who rejected the circumcision of the old covenant were cut off from the covenant. Certainly God is not going to condone rebellion and disobedience, even in our new covenant relationship.

Water baptism is a vital experience for repentant believers.

Here are some examples that show us the importance of this experience in God:

1. When the Holy Spirit was poured out on the Day of Pentecost, the crowd mocked them at first. Peter stood and preached to the people, and the Holy Spirit convicted their hearts. Then they cried out and said, "What shall we do?" Peter did not use indirect counseling. He did not ask, "What do you think you should do?" He said, "Repent, and be baptized every one of you" (Acts 2:37–38, KJV).

2. Philip the evangelist preached Jesus to an Ethiopian nobleman. The man was challenged by Philip's words and requested to be baptized. He considered it so important he was baptized by the side of the road—at once!

Now as they went down the road, they came to some water. And the eunuch said, "See, here is water. What hinders me from being baptized?" Then Philip said, "If you believe with all your heart, you may." And he answered and said, "I believe that Jesus Christ is the Son of God."

—ACTS 8:36–37

Baptism without faith is meaningless and accomplishes nothing.

3. When God, by an earthquake, delivered Paul and Silas from prison, the jailer was afraid for his life:

[He] said, "Sirs, what must I do to be saved?" So they said, "Believe on the Lord Jesus Christ, and you will be saved, you and your household." Then they spoke the word of the Lord to him and to all who were in his house. And he took them the same hour of the night and washed their stripes. And immediately he and all his family were baptized.

—ACTS 16:30–33

It was so important they did it in the middle of the night.

4. Saul of Tarsus believed and repented on the road to Damascus. A believer by the name of Ananias came to him on Straight Street in Damascus and said:

Receive your sight and be filled with the Holy Spirit.

—ACTS 9:17

And now why are you waiting? Arise and be baptized, and wash away your sins, calling on the name of the Lord.

—ACTS 22:16

The important factor here and in all acts of water baptism is not water. The key is faith, submission, and complete obedience to the truth of God's Word, combined with the operation of the Holy Spirit.

At this point, I want to deal with the subject of authority in water baptism. When we baptize believers, we believe with them for a powerful work of the Holy Spirit in their lives. We expect to see people changed, and we have been given this commission in the Word of God:

> And whatever you do in word or deed, do all in the name of the
> Lord Jesus, giving thanks to God the Father through Him.
> —COLOSSIANS 3:17

Through the years, a conflict has arisen concerning the formula used in water baptism. There is much argument and disagreement over the Godhead—the Father, Son, and Holy Spirit. I will not become involved in the Godhead argument for two reasons:

1. However God chooses to reveal Himself will be wonderful, and we will rejoice throughout all eternity because of His wisdom, His glory, His power, and especially His love. You may refer to the Godhead as three manifestations, personalities, or persons, and I will have no controversy with you as long as we are clear on the point of one God.

2. I have heard and read the words of some of the greatest theologians in the world—past and present—as they discussed and taught on this subject. Yet, I have never heard the Godhead adequately explained. I believe in the Father, Son, and Holy Spirit—but one God. God's Word says it is a mystery, and I will leave it there:

> And without controversy great is the mystery of godliness: God was manifested in the flesh, justified in the Spirit, seen by angels, preached among the Gentiles, believed on in the world, received up in glory.
> —1 TIMOTHY 3:16

However, I do have a belief concerning our authority in water baptism. It has nothing to do with the Godhead controversy, but it has a lot to do with the power that is in His name. Jesus told the disciples (the Twelve), "Go therefore and make disciples of all the nations, baptizing them in the name of the Father and of the Son and of the Holy Spirit" (Matthew 28:19).

These Twelve He left with full authority to carry out His words and His commission. They were close to Him. They had the advantage of being under His personal teaching for about three and one-half years. They correctly understood these words—Father, Son and Holy Spirit—

as being titles and relationships. On the Day of Pentecost, being full of the Holy Spirit and guided by Him, they carried out the divine command of the Lord.

When the people of Israel crossed through the Red Sea, the Bible says they were baptized and identified with their God-given leader. They "all were baptized into Moses in the cloud and in the sea" (1 Cor. 10:2).

Father God did not die. The Holy Spirit did not die. Jesus died, and we are identifying with Him in His death, burial, and Resurrection in our baptism. Therefore, our authority is in His name. Our identity is in His name. Remember Paul's words: "And whatever you do in word or deed, do all in the name of the Lord Jesus, giving thanks to God the Father through Him" (Col. 3:17).

As we look at the activity of the apostles after Jesus' ascension, there is not one incident in the Bible where the words of Matthew 28:19 are used, commanded, or even suggested as a formula in water baptism. I would like to close by giving four Bible witnesses concerning this truth called water baptism:

1. On the Day of Pentecost: "Then Peter said to them, 'Repent, and let every one of you be baptized in the name of Jesus Christ for the remission of sins; and you shall receive the gift of the Holy Spirit'" (Acts 2:38).

2. When Philip preached in Samaria, they were "baptized in the name of the Lord Jesus" (Acts 8:16).

3. At the house of Cornelius, the Gentiles were baptized in the Holy Spirit, and Peter "commanded them to be baptized in the name of the Lord" (Acts 10:48).

4. Paul, speaking to the Ephesian disciples of John the Baptist, instructed them in their responsibilities, and "When they heard this, they were baptized in the name of the Lord Jesus" (Acts 19:5).

WHAT ABOUT THE BLOOD?

As we close this chapter, we give honor to the One who died on the cross and shed His blood for us. We are not cleansed from sin by water. First

John 1:7 says it is the blood of Jesus that cleanses us from all sin. In water baptism, our act of faith and obedience brings us into covenant harmony with God.

I am sometimes asked, "Can I come into this covenant harmony with God by any other way?" My answer: "Possibly, but why ask such a question? Why consider some other alternative? God's Word is clear, so why not do it His way?" As for me, I will do it the "Bible way." I will teach it the "Bible way." Let us not look for loopholes.

Nevertheless, my final words are grace, mercy, and love. I am called to declare truth, but I am not called to condemn those who disagree. I am waiting for that day when we shall all see "eye to eye." In the meantime, I do not believe the formula for water baptism should be used to divide the body of Christ.

Chapter 15

THE BAPTISM OF THE HOLY SPIRIT

O NE OF THE most amazing things about God is that He wants to live among His people. He wants to be identified with mankind. He did it with Adam and Eve in the garden, and they ended up rejecting God and leading the whole world into the pit of sin.

God then called for Himself a special people, Israel. After Moses led them out of their Egyptian bondage, they went to a mountain called Sinai. Here God gave Moses the plans to build a tabernacle, known as "the tabernacle of Moses." Inside this tabernacle was a special room, commonly called the "holy of holies" (Exodus 26:33–34). The ark of the covenant was placed in this room. Two golden cherubim—angelic creatures—were on top of the ark, one at each end. God manifested His presence between these golden cherubim. He was living among His people.

Israel's response to this miraculous arrangement was almost unbelievable. They turned away from their true, covenant God to false gods. God withdrew His protection. Their enemies came in, defeated them, scattered them, and they lost the presence of God. No one knows what happened to the ark. The best information is that Nebuchadnezzar, king of Babylon, came and destroyed the temple of Solomon and much of Jerusalem. After that, we never hear of the earthly ark again. Without the presence of God, it had no more significance:

> And all the articles from the house of God, great and small, the treasures of the house of the Lord, and the treasures of the king and of his leaders, all these he took to Babylon. Then they burned the house of God, broke down the wall of Jerusalem, burned all its palaces with fire, and destroyed all its precious possessions.
>
> —2 CHRONICLES 36:18–19

God did not give up. The prophet Isaiah spoke of One who was coming to represent God:

> Therefore the Lord Himself will give you a sign: Behold, the virgin shall conceive and bear a Son, and shall call His name Immanuel.
>
> —ISAIAH 7:14

Jesus was the fulfillment of this prophecy. In describing the coming Messiah, an angel from God spoke these words concerning Mary, who was to be the mother of Jesus:

> And she will bring forth a Son, and you shall call His name JESUS, for He will save His people from their sins. So all this was done that it might be fulfilled which was spoken by the Lord through the prophet, saying: "Behold, the virgin shall be with child, and bear a Son, and they shall call His name Immanuel, which is translated, 'God with us.'"
>
> —MATTHEW 1:21–23

In the person of Jesus, the Christ, God was once again living among the human race. Paul said, "God was in Christ reconciling the world to Himself" (2 Cor 5:19). How glorious to have the God of creation walking among you! Yet, once again Israel and the world failed to take advantage of this opportunity. After Jesus had ministered three and one-half years, they crucified Him. "He came to His own, and His own did not receive Him" (John 1:11).

In spite of this awful act, God did not stop. He had a plan to rescue His people. He was determined, not just to live among them, but to live in them. The prophet Ezekiel had foretold what God was going to do:

> Then I will give them one heart, and I will put a new spirit within them, and take the stony heart out of their flesh, and give them a heart of flesh, that they may walk in My statutes and keep My judgments and do them; and they shall be My people, and I will be their God.
>
> —EZEKIEL 11:19–20

> I will put My Spirit within you and cause you to walk in My statutes, and you will keep My judgments and do them.
>
> —EZEKIEL 36:27

God was now promising to put His Spirit in His people. In this way, He was going to help them—actually cause them—to walk in obedience to God's Word and His will. Human ability had failed; now "God ability, Spirit ability" was going to empower them.

JESUS AND THE HOLY SPIRIT

Before Jesus ascended, He spoke of the coming of the Holy Spirit:

> When He, the Spirit of truth, has come, He will guide you into all truth; for He will not speak on His own authority, but whatever He hears He will speak; and He will tell you things to come. He will glorify Me, for He will take of what is Mine and declare it to you.
>
> —JOHN 16:13–14

We learn five important things about the Holy Spirit from these words of Jesus:

1. He will guide us into all truth. The same Holy Spirit who inspired the writers of the Scriptures will guide us in understanding their writings. He will also guide us in following Jesus, who is "the way, the truth, and the life" (John 14:6).

2. He shall not speak of Himself or on His own authority.

3. He will speak what He hears. The Holy Spirit knows the mind, the "code" of God. He has access to the heavenly scene, and He will translate God's message to us. He also knows what the devil is planning for us. If we will learn to listen, He will whisper to us, "Watch out, be careful."

4. He will show you things to come. We will never understand many mysteries about God, His Word, and our future without the indwelling presence of the Holy Spirit.

5. He will glorify and magnify Jesus.

Here is my paraphrase and understanding of John 16:13–14: "He shall (without prejudice) lead us into God's truth. He will properly relate that truth to Jesus Christ. He will use the revelation of that truth and the wisdom of that truth to prepare us for the future." What a glorious opportunity we have!

Having said all of this, it is now time for the big question:

Who Is the Holy Spirit?

First, He is the One who gave us the Bible. He is the Author of the Scriptures:

> No prophecy of Scripture is of any private interpretation, for prophecy never came by the will of man, but holy men of God spoke as they were moved by the Holy Spirit.
>
> —2 Peter 1:20–21

The Bible gives many descriptions, qualities, and attributes to explain the Holy Spirit. But as to who He is, there is only one answer: He is God. You might want to go back and review the chapter on God. In that chapter, we listed the four important attributes of God. These same attributes belong to the Holy Spirit.

When a man by the name of Ananias lied about his offering (gift) to Peter, the apostle said, "Ananias, why has Satan filled your heart to lie to the Holy Spirit...You have not lied to men but to God" (Acts 5:3–4). In lying to the Spirit-filled and Spirit-directed apostle, Ananias was lying to the Holy Spirit, and thus to God.

We learn more about the name Holy Spirit from the study of two words in the Bible. Hebrew is the language of the Old Testament; Greek is the language of the New Testament. The Hebrew word for Spirit is *Ruach*, meaning "wind, breath; expression of a rational being, including its expression and functions." The Greek word is *Pneuma*, meaning, "a current of air, wind, breath (blast), or a breeze."

The Bible gives many names to the Holy Spirit. He is called the "Spirit of truth" in John 16:13, the "Spirit of God and the Spirit of Christ" in Romans 8:9, the "Spirit of life" in Romans 8:2, the "Spirit of wisdom and understanding" in Isaiah 11:2. Jesus referred to Him as "the Comforter (One who comes alongside to help)":

> But the Helper [the Comforter], the Holy Spirit, whom the Father will send in My name, He will teach you all things, and bring to your remembrance all things that I said to you.
>
> —JOHN 14:26

We see the importance of the Holy Spirit in Jesus' words in John 4:24: "God is Spirit, and those who worship Him must worship in spirit and truth." Just before He went away, Jesus brought the apostles together for one last, earthly meeting:

> Therefore, when they had come together, they asked Him, saying "Lord, will You at this time restore the kingdom to Israel?" And He said to them, "It is not for you to know times or seasons which the Father has put in His own authority. But you shall receive power when the Holy Spirit has come upon you; and you shall be witnesses to Me in Jerusalem, and in all Judea and Samaria, and to the end of the earth."
>
> —ACTS 1:6–8

It is important that we clearly understand what is being discussed here. The disciples were asking about the kingdom of God. They had read the words of the prophets concerning the golden days of Israel during the time of David and Solomon. They were asking, "Lord, are you going to restore the glorious power and grandeur of the kingdom?" Here is my paraphrase of His answer: "I am not going to tell you the whole story now, but if you want power, here is the way it's going to happen. You will get power when the Holy Spirit comes upon you. As a result of that power, you are going to be my witnesses in Jerusalem, Judea, Samaria, and to the end of the earth." These words of Jesus came to pass on the Day of Pentecost when they were baptized in the Holy Spirit.

What Is This Baptism With the Holy Spirit?

This baptism in, with, or by the Holy Spirit is a baptism of the believer into and with the very Spirit of God, giving him or her unlimited power to do the works of Christ. The word *power* in Acts 1:8 is the Greek word *dunamis*. It means "force, miraculous activity or ability, an abundance of miracle strength." Our English word *dynamite* comes from this Greek word. With this power in our lives, a whole new world opens to us. Jesus said we would have power to witness for Him and about Him. But there is much more:

1. We will have the ability and understanding to truly worship God:

God is Spirit, and those who worship Him must worship in spirit and truth.

—John 4:24

[We] worship God in the Spirit, rejoice in Christ Jesus, and have no confidence in the flesh.

—Philippians 3:3

2. We will have the God-given ability to understand His instructions to us, especially through the Scriptures:

When He, the Spirit of truth, has come, He will guide you into all truth.

—John 16:13

Now we have received, not the spirit of the world, but the Spirit who is from God, that we might know the things that have been freely given to us by God.

—1 Corinthians 2:12

3. We will have the ability to hear from God, to know His voice

and receive guidance and direction for our lives. Jesus told His disciples:

> When they arrest you, do not worry about it. You will be given the right word to speak, but it won't be your word…it will be the Holy Spirit speaking through you.
> —MARK 13:11, AUTHOR'S PARAPHRASE

Barnabas and Saul had their ministries confirmed through the spoken word of the Holy Spirit:

> As they ministered to the Lord and fasted, the Holy Spirit said, "Now separate to Me Barnabas and Saul for the work to which I have called them."
> —ACTS 13:2

4. We will have power in prayer:

> Likewise the Spirit also helps in our weaknesses. For we do not know what we should pray for as we ought, but the Spirit Himself makes intercession for us with groanings which cannot be uttered. Now He who searches the hearts knows what the mind of the Spirit is, because He makes intercession for the saints according to the will of God.
> —ROMANS 8:26–27

5. We will have power and authority to exercise the spiritual gifts of 1 Corinthians, chapters 12 and 14.

6. We demonstrate our spiritual walk with God by the manifestation of the fruit of the Spirit. A person who is controlled by Satan will produce the "works of the flesh." When we are controlled by the Holy Spirit, we will manifest the "fruit of the Spirit." The word *fruit* is the Greek word *karpas* from *kara* (joy).

7. Galatians 5:22–23: "But the fruit [joyful production] of the Spirit is love, joy, peace, longsuffering, kindness, goodness, faithfulness, gentleness, self-control. Against such there is no law."

The Coming of the Holy Spirit
Was No Surprise!

Before He ascended to the throne of God, Jesus gave His disciples these instructions:

> And being assembled together with them, He commanded them not to depart from Jerusalem, but to wait for the Promise of the Father, "which," He said, "you have heard from Me; for John truly baptized with water, but you shall be baptized with the Holy Spirit not many days from now."
>
> —Acts 1:4–5

This was not the first time the coming of the Holy Spirit had been promised. The prophets of the Old Testament had already spoken of the great phenomenon that was coming:

> For I will take you from among the nations, gather you out of all countries, and bring you into your own land. Then I will sprinkle clean water on you, and you shall be clean; I will cleanse you from all your filthiness and from all your idols. I will give you a new heart and put a new spirit within you; I will take the heart of stone out of your flesh and give you a heart of flesh. I will put My Spirit within you and cause you to walk in My statutes, and you will keep My judgments and do them.
>
> —Ezekiel 36:24–27

> And it shall come to pass afterward that I will pour out My Spirit on all flesh; your sons and your daughters shall prophesy, your old men shall dream dreams, your young men shall see visions. And also on My menservants and on My maidservants I will pour out My Spirit in those days.
>
> —Joel 2:28–29

These prophetic words were fulfilled on the Day of Pentecost:

> When the Day of Pentecost had fully come, they were all with one accord in one place. And suddenly there came a sound from heaven, as of a rushing mighty wind, and it filled the whole house

where they were sitting. Then there appeared to them divided tongues, as of fire, and one sat upon each of them. And they were all filled with the Holy Spirit and began to speak with other tongues, as the Spirit gave them utterance.

—ACTS 2:1–4

[When the people of Jerusalem saw and heard this, they said,] "They are full of [drunk with] new wine." But Peter...said to them, "...this is what was spoken by the prophet Joel."

—ACTS 2:13–16

REVIEWING THE ETERNAL PLAN OF GOD

- God became involved with mankind by Creation, fellowshiping with them, shedding the light of His presence around them, and imparting His wisdom and authority to them.

- Man rebelled and walked from God's light into sinful darkness. God sent messengers—priests, prophets, and kings to the human race, blessing them abundantly. Yet they continued in their rebellion against God until finally, they could no longer hear His voice or see His light.

- Into this darkness and sinful confusion came a Man—Jesus, the Savior, Messiah, and King. In Him, God had come to live among His people and bring His light into their lives. This Jesus was the Pivot Point, the Link, the Mediator between God and mankind (us):

Then Jesus spoke to them again, saying, "I am the light of the world. He who follows Me shall not walk in darkness, but have the light of life."

—JOHN 8:12

For there is one God and one Mediator between God and men, the Man Christ Jesus.

—1 TIMOTHY 2:5

153

- Once again, the people rejected God's plan to live among them. When they crucified the Lord of glory, it would seem God had totally failed—but not so! After the death, burial, and Resurrection of Jesus from the grave, He was ready to ascend to the throne. Before He left His followers, He gave this command in Luke 24:49: "Behold, I send the Promise of My Father upon you; but tarry [wait] in the city of Jerusalem until you are endued with power from on high."

- The Holy Spirit was coming to "abide" with them forever (John 14:16). God would live in His people! On the Day of Pentecost, this promise was fulfilled, and nothing would ever be the same again!

THIS "BAPTISM IN THE HOLY SPIRIT" IS AVAILABLE TODAY

It would be tragic if this wonderful experience had disappeared with the last apostle or if it were only available for a short time. Our needs are great, and we need all the help we can get. We need the power of the Holy Spirit in our lives.

Peter stood before the multitude on the Day of Pentecost and preached one of the greatest sermons the world has ever known. His words were so powerful, so right, so compelling that the people cried out, "What shall we do?" Then Peter said to them, "Repent, and let every one of you be baptized in the name of Jesus Christ for the remission of sins; and you shall receive the gift of the Holy Spirit" (Acts 2:37–38).

All they had to do was to become obedient—just do it! Many of them obeyed Peter's words. They believed, they repented, they were baptized, they received the glorious Holy Spirit into their lives. This same experience is for us today:

> "For the promise is to you and to your children, and to all who are afar off, as many as the Lord our God will call." And with many other words he [Peter] testified and exhorted them, saying, "Be saved from this perverse generation." Then those who gladly received his word were baptized; and that day about three thousand souls were added to them.
>
> —ACTS 2:39–41

Many signs accompany the Spirit-filled life. The initial sign of being baptized in/with/by the Holy Spirit is revealed in Acts 2:4: "They were all filled with the Holy Spirit and began to speak with other tongues, as the Spirit gave them utterance."

Today, many people have objections to this miraculous manifestation of the Holy Spirit. These objections can be summed up in two major points:

1. Since the Day of Pentecost, all believers are automatically baptized in the Holy Spirit at the time of conversion, when they believe on Jesus.

2. "Tongues" are not for today, and they were only given in New Testament times because the church did not have the Bible. The tongues were languages God used to preach the gospel to people who did not otherwise understand.

BIBLE ANSWERS TO MAN'S OBJECTIONS

The Bible records four major times when groups of people were baptized in the Holy Spirit.

1. At Pentecost

And they were all filled with the Holy Spirit and began to speak with other tongues, as the Spirit gave them utterance...Now when they heard this, they were cut to the heart, and said to Peter and the rest of the apostles, "Men and brethren, what shall we do?" Then Peter said to them, "Repent, and let every one of you be baptized in the name of Jesus Christ for the remission of sins; and you shall receive the gift of the Holy Spirit. For the promise is to you and to your children, and to all who are afar off, as many as the Lord our God will call."

—ACTS 2:4, 37–39

This was the initial outpouring. Here, the people believed, repented, were baptized, and received the gift of the Holy Spirit. It seems that people either totally rejected Peter's words or wholly accepted them and acted upon them. This is the pattern for people coming to God.

Tongues were not needed to preach the gospel. The Greek language was universal in the days of the New Testament. Peter had already preached to the people in a language they understood. They were already convicted of their need for God. That is why they asked, "What shall we do?"

2. At Samaria

> But when they believed Philip as he preached the things concerning the kingdom of God and the name of Jesus Christ, both men and women were baptized...Now when the apostles who were at Jerusalem heard that Samaria had received the word of God, they sent Peter and John to them, who, when they had come down, prayed for them that they might receive the Holy Spirit. For as yet He had fallen upon none of them. They had only been baptized in the name of the Lord Jesus. Then they laid hands on them, and they received the Holy Spirit.
>
> —ACTS 8:12, 14–17

They had believed and were baptized, but they had not yet received the Holy Spirit experience. So we understand that everybody does not receive everything at once.

Neither Philip nor the apostles had to use "miracle tongues" to preach the gospel. In fact, at this one place only, nothing is said about their speaking in tongues. However, we know that something unusual—either visually or audibly—happened. If not, why would Simon have been willing to pay money to bestow the gift upon others?

> And when Simon saw that through the laying on of the apostles' hands the Holy Spirit was given, he offered them money, saying, "Give me this power also, that anyone on whom I lay hands may receive the Holy Spirit."
>
> —ACTS 8:18–19

3. Cornelius with Peter

> While Peter was still speaking these words, the Holy Spirit fell upon all those who heard the word. And those of the circumcision [Jewish believers] who believed were astonished, as many as came with Peter, because the gift of the Holy Spirit had been

poured out on the Gentiles also. For they heard them speak with tongues and magnify God.

—Acts 10:44–46

Cornelius had already been praying and had received word from God to send for Peter. Then, as Peter told them of Jesus, they began to believe. Suddenly, and in God's sovereign power, the Holy Spirit was poured out on them.

Tongues were not needed to preach the gospel. Peter had already been preaching to them in a language they understood. However, the Jews that came with Peter knew the "gift of the Holy Spirit had been poured out on the Gentiles... For they heard them speak with tongues." This was the initial sign; this was the first evidence.

4. Ephesus with Paul and the disciples

[Paul came to Ephesus and found some disciples who had believed.]...he said to them, "Did you receive the Holy Spirit when you believed?" So they said to him, "We have not so much as heard whether there is a Holy Spirit." And he said to them, "Into what then were you baptized?" So they said, "Into John's baptism." Then Paul said, "John indeed baptized with a baptism of repentance, saying to the people that they should believe on Him who would come after him, that is, on Christ Jesus." When they heard this, they were baptized in the name of the Lord Jesus. And when Paul had laid hands on them, the Holy Spirit came upon them, and they spoke with tongues and prophesied.

—Acts 19:2–6

When John the Baptist told his disciples about Jesus ("Behold! The Lamb of God who takes away the sin of the world!" [John 1:29]), they had believed. But they had not yet been water baptized, nor had they received the outpouring of the Holy Spirit. Everything did not come at once.

Tongues were not needed to preach the gospel. The Ephesians were Greeks, and Paul was fluent in their language. He laid hands on them, the Holy Spirit came upon them, and they "spoke with tongues and prophesied" (Acts 19:6).

When the Bible says they "prophesied," it does not mean they were "preaching the gospel." The Greek word *propheteuo* is used here, meaning, "to foretell events, speaking under divine inspiration, exercising the prophetic gift." The expression "preach the word" is mentioned twice in the New Testament. In Acts 16:6, the word is *laleo*, meaning "utter words, preach, speak, talk and tell." In 2 Timothy 4:2, the word is *kerusso*, meaning "to herald, especially divine truth, preach, and publish."

How Shall We Receive This Experience?

At Pentecost, the Holy Spirit came to stay. His coming was a sovereign outpouring from God. Today we can read and believe the Word of God, or we can believe the preaching of the gospel, and the same thing can happen to us.

At Samaria, the Holy Spirit came with the ministry of the "laying-on of hands." We shall study about this in our next chapter.

At the house of Cornelius, the Holy Spirit was poured out when they heard and believed the Word being preached.

At Ephesus, the Holy Spirit was poured out when hands were laid on them. It is not necessary that the laying-on of hands be ministered by an apostle. Saul of Tarsus received the Holy Spirit when "a certain disciple at Damascus named Ananias" laid hands on him (Acts 9:10). As far as we know from the Bible, he was neither an apostle nor a prophet. He was a disciple—a follower of Jesus. If you want to receive this baptism in the Holy Spirit, here are some suggestions:

1. Pray and ask God for His wonderful gift:

If you then, being evil, know how to give good gifts to your children, how much more will your heavenly Father give the Holy Spirit to those who ask Him!

—Luke 11:13

2. Enter into God's presence with thanksgiving, praise, and worship. Open your mouth and begin to "drink" of the Spirit of God:

Enter into His gates with thanksgiving, and into His courts with praise. Be thankful to Him, and bless [adore, praise, thank] His name.

—Psalm 100:4

On the last day, that great day of the feast, Jesus stood and cried out, saying, "If anyone thirsts, let him come to Me and drink. He who believes in Me, as the Scripture has said, out of his heart will flow rivers of living water." But this He spoke concerning the Spirit, whom those believing in Him would receive.

—JOHN 7:37–39

3. While we are "drinking" of the Spirit, anointed and God-cleansed hands should be laid upon us. Faith is important. We must have faith, and the person(s) laying hands on us must have faith to believe the Word of God:

Then they laid hands on them, and they received the Holy Spirit.

—ACTS 8:17

4. As the Holy Spirit comes upon us, we must yield our thoughts and our speech to the Lord, allowing the Spirit of God to speak through us. The words will be foreign to our understanding, but this is the "tongues sign" of the Holy Spirit baptism:

And they were all filled with the Holy Spirit and began to speak with other tongues, as the Spirit gave them utterance. [They spoke with the Spirit's ability.]

—ACTS 2:4

We will speak more about tongues in a future chapter on prayer, praise, and worship. Now, we close this chapter with five negatives or problems—the reasons that more people do not receive this wonderful experience from God. We can do something about each of them:

- Lack of commitment—We can change our attitude and say yes to God's way for us.

- Sin, pride, and rebellion—We can repent and surrender to God's will.

- Unbelief—Faith comes by hearing the Word of God. Get into the Bible and a good church.

- Ignorance—We can study God's Word, believe it, and receive it into our lives.

- Fear—"God has not given us a spirit of fear" (2 Tim. 1:7).

One of the most powerful blessings given to the church is the ministry of the laying-on of hands. There is an impartation and a confirmation that happens when this ministry is used in obedience to God's Word. This is not some unusual or new teaching. It was started in the Old Testament and continued in the activity and teaching of the New Testament church. In fact, this ministry is listed as one of the foundational principles of the "doctrine of Christ" in Hebrews 6:1–2:

> Therefore, leaving the discussion of the elementary principles of Christ, let us go on to perfection, not laying again the foundation of repentance from dead works and of faith toward God, of the doctrine of baptisms, of laying on of hands, of resurrection of the dead, and of eternal judgment.

The Laying-On of Hands and Healing

In any doctrine, teaching, or practice, it is always wise to look at the life, ministry, and teachings of Jesus and the apostles to see what we might learn. On the subject of the laying-on of hands for healing, we learn a great deal. Simon Peter had a wife, and his wife's mother was sick. Jesus healed her, and then we read these words:

> When the sun was setting, all those who had any that were sick with various diseases brought them to Him; and He laid His hands on every one of them and healed them.
>
> —Luke 4:40

> [The apostles also laid hands on the sick.] And through the hands of the apostles many signs and wonders were done among the people. And they were all with one accord in Solomon's Porch.
>
> —Acts 5:12

And it happened that the father of Publius lay sick of a fever and dysentery. Paul went in to him and prayed, and he laid his hands on him and healed him.

—Acts 28:8

True believers in the Lord Jesus Christ have the authority to lay hands on the sick for healing:

And these signs will follow those who believe: In My name...they will lay hands on the sick, and they will recover.

—Mark 16:17–18

Many years ago, scientists and members of the medical profession scoffed at the thought of laying hands upon a patient for strength, encouragement, and healing. Today this has changed. Publications from many highly credible institutions encourage prayer and the laying-on of hands for their patients. They believe this will help the healing process.

There was also a time when many religious groups spoke harshly against the medical profession. They believed that if they consulted a physician, they were showing signs of unbelief. Now we know that "every good gift...is from above" (James 1:17). We thank God for the dedication of doctors, nurses, medical technicians, and hospital personnel. We know many physicians and doctors of dental surgery who lay hands on their patients and pray for them before they begin the medical and surgical process. Thank God that ministers, believers, and medical teams can work together to bring blessing to many.

The laying-on of hands for the receiving of the baptism in the Holy Spirit was often done in the Bible, and we have already done extensive teaching on this subject.

Chapter 16

THE LAYING-ON
OF HANDS

THE BLESSINGS OF CONFIRMATION

THE MINISTRY OF blessing, impartation, and confirmation was an important part of the New Testament Church ministry. These scriptures confirm this:

And when they had preached the gospel to that city and made many disciples, they returned to Lystra, Iconium, and Antioch, strengthening [confirming, supporting, and reestablishing] the souls of the disciples, exhorting them to continue in the faith, and saying, "We must through many tribulations enter the kingdom of God."

—ACTS 14:21–22

Now Judas and Silas, themselves being prophets also, exhorted and strengthened [confirmed] the brethren with many words.

—ACTS 15:32

And he [Paul] went through Syria and Cilicia, strengthening [confirming] the churches.

—ACTS 15:41

We have explained the change of attitude about the medical profession and divine healing. In the same sense, many religious groups were once adamant against the laying-on of hands with prophetic utterance. Now this has also changed. Today denominational and nondenominational groups all over the world are not only open to this ministry, but they are actively inviting teams of prophetic presbyters (apostles and prophets) into their churches and conferences.

When we discuss impartation and confirmation, we do not want to put God in a box. This ministry can come to us in different ways. We start with the most basic way. We can receive blessing from God, a call from God, or the confirmation of that call by reading God's Word and putting it into operation in our life.

The call, the confirmation, and direction from God can also come to every believer as the Holy Spirit speaks to our hearts, saying, "This is the way; walk in it" (Isa. 30:21). Nevertheless, there were specific times in the Bible when God used prophetic ministry, sometimes with the laying-on of hands, and at other times, the prophetic alone. At these times, special gifts and enabling were imparted, and ministries were confirmed in the lives of God's servants. It is not my purpose to deal fully with the following examples, but merely to point out that it did happen.

OLD TESTAMENT EXAMPLES OF PROPHETIC CONFIRMATION

1. *Jacob spoke prophetic words to his children and grandchildren.*
   Before Jacob died, he called his children together. He laid his hands on them, giving them prophetic words concerning their future and the future of Israel as a nation (Gen. 48:13–22, 49:1–28).

2. *Moses ordained Joshua to be Israel's new leader.*

   - In Deuteronomy 1:38, God gave Moses the word that Joshua was to be the new leader.

- In Deuteronomy 3:28, Moses spoke to Joshua words concerning his future.

- In Deuteronomy 31:7, 23, Moses spoke to Joshua before all Israel. Here is the result:

Now Joshua the son of Nun was full of the spirit of wisdom, for Moses had laid his hands on him; so the children of Israel heeded him, and did as the Lord had commanded Moses.

—Deuteronomy 34:9

3. *Elisha spoke prophetic words of revelation to Israel's king.* Elisha the prophet was on his deathbed. He called Joash, King of Israel to him and prophesied about the battles and victories he would have against the nation of Syria (2 Kings 13:14–19).

4. *Isaiah prophesied King Hezekiah's death—and then his healing.* When Hezekiah cried to the Lord after Isaiah's prophetic word that he would die, Isaiah gave Hezekiah another word that God would give him fifteen more years (Isa. 38:1–8).

5. *The people prospered through the prophetic words of Haggai and Zechariah.* A remnant of people were permitted to leave the land of their captivity and return to Jerusalem to rebuild the temple and the walls at Jerusalem. The words of these prophets brought great encouragement to this group:

So the elders of the Jews built, and they prospered through the prophesying of Haggai the prophet and Zechariah the son of Iddo. And they built and finished it, according to the commandment of the God of Israel.

—Ezra 6:14

New Testament Examples of Prophetic Confirmation

1. *When Mary and Joseph brought the baby Jesus to the temple.* At this time, an old man by the name of Simeon and an old

woman by the name of Anna confirmed the validity of the Christ child. Their words also prepared Mary for difficult days ahead (Luke 2:25–38).

2. *The confirmation of God's call upon Barnabas and Saul at the church in Antioch.* It is obvious that these two already knew they were called of God. The Holy Spirit spoke and confirmed it to the church and to the world (Acts 13:1–4).

3. *The life and call of Timothy was greatly blessed by the ministry of the laying-on of hands and prophecy.* There are three Bible references:

This charge I commit to you, son Timothy, according to the prophecies previously made concerning you, that by them you may wage the good warfare.

—1 TIMOTHY 1:18

Do not neglect the gift that is in you, which was given to you by prophecy with the laying on of the hands of the eldership.

—1 TIMOTHY 4:14

Therefore I remind you to stir up the gift of God which is in you through the laying on of my hands.

—2 TIMOTHY 1:6

HOW DOES THIS MINISTRY WORK IN THE CHURCH TODAY?

When God's people prepare their hearts to hear from God, it is better that a presbytery be involved. The word *presbytery* comes from the Greek word *presbutaros*, meaning "elder." The elders must be prophets, apostles, and ministers with a proven prophetic ministry.

Confirmation, with the laying-on of hands and prophecy, should not ordinarily come to new believers. God's people should first offer themselves for a time of training and intense study of the Word of God. That is one of the purposes of this book. When this course has been completed, it is time for us to make ourselves available for service in the church. Every believer should expect to have a ministry and to have that ministry confirmed by God. This often happens through the systematic study of God's Word, together with godly counseling from an experienced, credible pastor and leader. At other times a presbytery is involved. This is what happened to Timothy.

The Bible teaches that confirmation should come to those who are being ordained into a full-time ministry. We believe every ministry candidate should come before a mature presbytery that would include a prophetic ministry. This is what happened to Barnabas and Saul at Antioch:

> Now in the church that was at Antioch there were certain prophets and teachers: Barnabas, Simeon who was called Niger, Lucius of Cyrene, Manaen who had been brought up with Herod the tetrarch, and Saul. As they ministered to the Lord and fasted, the Holy Spirit said, "Now separate to Me Barnabas and Saul for the work to which I have called them." Then, having fasted and prayed, and laid hands on them, they sent them away.
>
> —ACTS 13:1–3

During the ministry of the laying-on of hands and prophecy, there is often the impartation of spiritual gifts and confirmation of ministries. This impartation and confirmation are by the sovereign work of the Holy Spirit. Man, in his own power, cannot give or impart these gifts, but the Holy Spirit does use yielded and prophetic vessels to make known the will of God.

MINISTRY TO BABIES AND CHILDREN

One final and important part of the laying-on of hands is the dedication and blessing of babies and children. It is not scriptural to baptize infants. The Bible teaches that we must repent and believe the gospel before our water baptism. An infant is not capable of doing this.

Nevertheless, through and by the laying-on of hands, children are dedicated and blessed (sanctified) unto the Lord Jesus Christ. Mary and Joseph brought the baby Jesus to the temple to present Him before God. This is a good example to follow.

Parents and guardians bear a great responsibility in this act of dedication. They are committing themselves to rear the children in the house of God, under the authority of the Word of God. By this dedication, their children are committed to God's protection, guidance, and blessing:

Then they brought little children to Him, that He might touch them; but the disciples rebuked those who brought them. But when Jesus saw it, He was greatly displeased and said to them, "Let the little children come to Me, and do not forbid them; for of such is the kingdom of God. Assuredly, I say to you, whoever does not receive the kingdom of God as a little child will by no means enter it." And He took them up in His arms, put His hands on them, and blessed them.

—MARK 10:13–16

In this dramatic incident, we see the great importance Jesus gave to children and their place in the kingdom of God.

THE BLESSINGS OF CONFIRMATION ARE MANY

We have learned experientially, in practical reality, the great blessings of this ministry. Through the laying-on of hands and prophecy, people are strengthened, encouraged, and established in the faith. Often, we hear new assurances of the truths we have studied and received, and we receive greater assurance of God's will and purposes for our lives.

Just as Joshua received a word from God through Moses, the same thing can happen to us. We can receive direction for our lives and ministries. This will usually begin when we accept new responsibilities in the local assembly.

We believe this ministry should be done before the local church. In this way, our ministry, gifts, and callings can be acknowledged by everyone who is part of the assembly, the church. This adds great credibility to us and to the ministry for which we have been called. This is not something to be done in home meetings or in a private or secret ministry where there is no local church leadership.

Finally, we must understand that this ministry often has been abused and some good people have been led astray. In the same sense, the presentation of the gospel often has been flawed and preached by unscrupulous people; but we must not discard or reject either the gospel or the laying-on of hands ministry for that reason. What we must do is join ourselves to a good local church with a credible "track record" of teaching and establishing its people in the truths of God's Word. Then we can prosper through this laying-on of hands ministry.

Chapter 17

RESURRECTION

AND

ETERNAL JUDGMENT

J UST AS CERTAINLY as we must wake up every morning and face the fact of living our lives, we must also face the fact of our death. The Bible says every one of us must die, and after that, face the judgment (Heb. 9:27).

Through the ages, the very thought of death brought terror to many people, and they lived their whole lifetime in bondage because of the fear of death. The real problem was this: death was a mystery, and they had no idea what was going to happen after they died.

When Jesus came, everything changed. Jesus died on the cross and paid the penalty for all our sins. Three days later, He was resurrected from the dead. His promise to the disciples and to us is this: "Because I live, you will live also" (John 14:19). When we receive Jesus as our Savior, we receive salvation and eternal life. The devil no longer has any claim on our lives, and we should have no fear concerning our future. We should love life, but not fear death.

Through His death, burial, and resurrection, Jesus came to "destroy him who had the power of death, that is, the devil, and release those who through fear of death were all their lifetime subject to bondage" (Heb. 2:14–15).

A Question From a Man Named Job

In the midst of all his troubles, Job began to think about the future after death. In Job 14:7–9, he said, "You can cut down a tree. The stump will die in the ground, but let a little water hit it, and buds will spring forth. The plant will live again" (my paraphrase). Then, in Job 14:10, 14, he asked the big question:

> But man dies and is laid away; indeed he breathes his last and where is he?...If a man dies, shall he live again?

This is the question of the ages. It is as old as the first grave. Multitudes have been filled with anguish as they stood at a grave. They want to believe. They are asking, "Will my loved one or my friend live again?" Adam and Eve must have stood by the grave of Abel with the same question. "If a man dies, shall he live again?" Will it really happen? Can we really have hope?

One thing is for certain: the man or woman without God does not have a bright future. The Bible is clear. There will be a resurrection, and "the last enemy that will be destroyed is death" (1 Cor. 15:26).

Even the "Natural Man" Cries Out "Yes!" to This Question

An inner feeling within mankind, even when he is not religious, says yes to the resurrection.

- In the tombs of Egypt, books were left for the dead to read in another life. People who believed in life after death put them there.

- Ancient warriors of European countries were buried with their armor so they could fight more battles in the next life.

- American Indians of olden days were buried with their bows and arrows.

The great majority of the scientific world was once in unbelief, but many have changed their minds. They now believe there is more than we can see with the natural eye and perceive with the natural mind. One of the scientists who mapped the pattern of DNA for the first time said that we are now seeing things that until this time have only been seen by God.

Man has an innate "knowing" that there is life after death. We are made too wonderfully and we have too much knowledge, love, and compassion for it to be wasted on eternal oblivion. We have an understanding that says, "This is not the end! The real me is not dirt and bone and hair, but a soul and a spirit that will live on."

Ralph Wilkerson, the author of *Beyond and Back*, interviewed scores of people who had experienced, "death, out-of-the-body experiences" and then returned to life again. In his book he tells the miraculous experiences of people who died and then returned to life. They did not know each other, yet their stories are remarkably similar.[1]

The Testimony of Bible Characters

The great King David, who was prophet, priest, and king, gave this testimony:

> But God will redeem my soul from the power of the grave, for He shall receive me.
>
> —Psalm 49:15

Hear these words from Daniel the prophet:

> And many of those who sleep in the dust of the earth shall awake, some to everlasting life, some to shame and everlasting contempt. Those who are wise shall shine like the brightness of the firmament, and those who turn many to righteousness like the stars forever and ever.
>
> —Daniel 12:2–3

Job, although he went through great pressure and suffering, never lost his faith:

For I know that my Redeemer lives, and He shall stand at last on the earth; and after my skin is destroyed, this I know, that in my flesh I shall see God.

—JOB 19:25–26

JESUS AND THE APOSTLES MADE THE RESURRECTION THE CENTRAL THEME OF THE GOSPEL

Jesus spoke these powerful words:

Do not marvel at this; for the hour is coming in which all who are in the graves will hear His voice and come forth—those who have done good, to the resurrection of life, and those who have done evil, to the resurrection of condemnation.

—JOHN 5:28–29

And this is the will of Him who sent Me, that everyone who sees the Son and believes in Him may have everlasting life; and I will raise him up at the last day.

—JOHN 6:40

Jesus came to show the way for all of us. The central theme of the gospel is the fact of Jesus' Resurrection from the dead. The apostles never missed an opportunity to declare it. "And with great power the apostles gave witness to the resurrection of the Lord Jesus" (Acts 4:33).

Without the Resurrection of Jesus from the grave, there would have been no "power." In fact, the very proof of His deity (His "God-ship") is in the Resurrection. Paul says, "[Jesus is] . . . declared to be the Son of God with power according to the Spirit of holiness, by the resurrection from the dead" (Rom. 1:4).

Not only does His Resurrection prove He is the Son of God, but without this Resurrection, there would be no salvation:

But if there is no resurrection of the dead, then Christ is not risen. And if Christ is not risen, then our preaching is empty and your faith is also empty.

—1 CORINTHIANS 15:13–14

> If you confess with your mouth the Lord Jesus and believe in your heart that God has raised Him from the dead, you will be saved.
>
> —Romans 10:9

The "Gospel" Includes the Resurrection

The teaching of the Resurrection is part of the gospel. Many people declare that the gospel is the story of the cross and the shedding of His blood that pays the penalty for all our sins. This is most important, but it is not the sum total of the gospel. If Jesus had not risen from the dead, it would all be meaningless, of no significance. There would be no "good news." Here in 1 Corinthians 15 is Paul's testimony on the subject of the gospel:

> Moreover, brethren, I declare to you the gospel which I preached to you, which also you received and in which you stand, by which also you are saved, if you hold fast that word which I preached to you—unless you believed in vain. For I delivered to you first of all that which I also received: that Christ died for our sins according to the Scriptures, and that He was buried, and that He rose again the third day according to the Scriptures, [1–4: This is part of the gospel message.]

> And if Christ is not risen, your faith is futile; you are still in your sins! [17]

> And if we have hope in Christ only for this life, we are the most miserable people in the world. But the fact is that Christ has been raised from the dead. He has become the first of a great harvest of those who will be raised to life again. For since by man [Adam] came death, by Man [Jesus] also came the resurrection of the dead. For as in Adam all die, even so in Christ all shall be made alive. But each one in his own order: Christ the first fruits, afterward those who are Christ's at His coming. [19–23, author's paraphrase]

> So also is the resurrection of the dead. The body is sown in corruption, it is raised in incorruption. It is sown in dishonor, it is raised in glory. It is sown in weakness, it is raised in power. It is

sown a natural body, it is raised a spiritual body. There is a natural body, and there is a spiritual body. [42–44]

Behold, I tell you a mystery: We shall not all sleep, but we shall all be changed—in a moment, in the twinkling of an eye, at the last trumpet. For the trumpet will sound, and the dead will be raised incorruptible, and we shall be changed. For this corruptible must put on incorruption, and this mortal must put on immortality. So when this corruptible has put on incorruption, and this mortal has put on immortality, then shall be brought to pass the saying that is written: "Death is swallowed up in victory." [51–54]
—1 CORINTHIANS 15:1–4, 17, 19–23, 42–44, 51–54

I love these beautiful words from the prophet Isaiah:

He will swallow up death forever, and the Lord God will wipe away tears from all faces.
—ISAIAH 25:8

THE TESTIMONY OF JESUS ABOUT HIMSELF

Finally, the confession of Jesus Himself tells the story. Speaking to Martha—whose brother, Lazarus, had died—Jesus said, "I am the resurrection and the life. He who believes in Me, though he may die, he shall live" (John 11:25).

Does this mean people will no longer die? No, but death is no longer of fearful significance! In our natural life, we are not afraid to go to sleep because we know we will wake up. The same is true with death. We go to sleep here; we wake up in His presence:

For we walk by faith, not by sight. We are confident, yes, well pleased rather to be absent from the body and to be present with the Lord.
—2 CORINTHIANS 5:7–8

And this is the will of Him who sent Me, that everyone who sees the Son and believes in Him may have everlasting life; and I will raise him up at the last day.
—JOHN 6:40

Three Types of Resurrection in the Bible

1. The Resurrection of Jesus Christ:

He is not here; for He is risen, as He said. Come, see the place where the Lord lay.

—Matthew 28:6

2. Resurrection life (our salvation experience) we can experience now:

And you, being dead in your trespasses and the uncircumcision of your flesh, He has made alive together with Him, having forgiven you all trespasses.

—Colossians 2:13

3. The resurrection of all the dead when Jesus returns:

Do not marvel at this; for the hour is coming in which all who are in the graves will hear His voice and come forth—those who have done good, to the resurrection of life, and those who have done evil, to the resurrection of condemnation.

—John 5:28–29

Paul's Words to the People of Thessalonica

Some of the people from the church at Thessalonica saw their loved ones dying, and their hearts were heavy. How unfortunate that their father, mother, sister, brother, or friends would not live to see the Resurrection. Paul wrote these words to set the record straight:

But I do not want you to be ignorant, brethren, concerning those who have fallen asleep, lest you sorrow as others who have no hope. For if we believe that Jesus died and rose again, even so God will bring with Him those who sleep in Jesus. For this we say to you by the word of the Lord, that we who are alive and remain until the coming of the Lord will by no means precede those who are asleep. For the Lord Himself will descend from heaven with a shout, with the voice of an archangel, and with the trumpet of

God. And the dead in Christ will rise first. Then we who are alive and remain shall be caught up together with them in the clouds to meet the Lord in the air. And thus we shall always be with the Lord. Therefore comfort one another with these words.

—1 THESSALONIANS 4:13–18

The words translated "sleep" and "asleep" come from the Greek word *koimao*, meaning "to sleep, be dead."

BIBLE FACTS CONCERNING THE RESURRECTION

1. Jesus is revealed as the Son of God with power, "by the resurrection from the dead" (Rom. 1:4).

2. Jesus came first as our Savior. When He returns, it will be as Judge:

For the Father judges no one, but has committed all judgment to the Son.

—JOHN 5:22

For we must all appear before the judgment seat of Christ, that each one may receive the things done in the body, according to what he has done, whether good or bad.

—2 CORINTHIANS 5:10

3. Believers are "in Christ." We will not be judged concerning our salvation, but our works will be judged:

Each one's work will become clear; for the Day will declare it, because it will be revealed by fire; and the fire will test each one's work, of what sort it is. If anyone's work which he has built on it [the proper foundation] endures, he will receive a reward. If anyone's work is burned, he will suffer loss; but he himself will be saved, yet so as through fire.

—1 CORINTHIANS 3:13–15

4. Paul says we will be "caught up…in the clouds to meet the Lord" and that we will "always be with the Lord" (1 Thess.

4:17). It is not God's plan that we will live in the clouds forever. We will meet Him, escort Him back to the earth, and it is on the "new earth" that we shall reign with Him. The Bible tells us that Jesus redeemed us to God by [His] blood:

Out of every tribe and tongue and people and nation, and [has] made us kings and priests to our God; and we shall reign on the earth.

—REVELATION 5:9–10

5. At the resurrection, when unbelievers face Jesus Christ on Judgment Day, they will already be condemned because they have rejected the Son of God:

He who believes in Him is not condemned; but he who does not believe is condemned already, because he has not believed in the name of the only begotten Son of God.

—JOHN 3:18

BIBLE FACTS ABOUT THE JUDGMENT— HELL AND HEAVEN

1. Hell was not made for human beings. In the beginning, hell was prepared only for the devil and the rebellious angels that followed him. Then, when man rebelled against God, he also chose hell instead of God's plan for heaven:

And do not fear those who kill the body but cannot kill the soul. But rather fear Him who is able to destroy both soul and body in hell.

—MATTHEW 10:28

Then He will also say to those on the left hand [these are human beings], "Depart from Me, you cursed, into the everlasting fire prepared for the devil and his angels."

—MATTHEW 25:41

2. Hell is no mystery. The Bible's information is most descriptive:

[Jesus said] There will be weeping and gnashing of teeth, when you see Abraham and Isaac and Jacob and all the prophets in the kingdom of God, and yourselves [religious hypocrites] thrust out [into hell].

—LUKE 13:28

The devil, who deceived them, was cast into the lake of fire and brimstone where the beast and the false prophet are. And they will be tormented day and night forever and ever.

—REVELATION 20:10

But the cowardly, unbelieving, abominable, murderers, sexually immoral, sorcerers, idolaters, and all liars shall have their part in the lake which burns with fire and brimstone.

—REVELATION 21:8

3. No one will have a chance to repent and get right with God after death. We have our opportunity to accept Jesus now. There will be no second chance after death:

He who believes in the Son has everlasting life; and he who does not believe the Son shall not see life, but the wrath of God abides on him.

—JOHN 3:36

And as it is appointed for men to die once, but after this the judgment.

—HEBREWS 9:27

Then the Lord knows how to deliver the godly out of temptations and to reserve the unjust under punishment for the day of judgment.

—2 PETER 2:9

BIBLE FACTS ABOUT HEAVEN

1. Great judgment is coming upon this earth, and there will be "a new heaven and a new earth":

> Now I saw a new heaven and a new earth, for the first heaven and the first earth had passed away. Also there was no more sea. Then I, John, saw the holy city, New Jerusalem, coming down out of heaven from God, prepared as a bride adorned for her husband.
>
> —REVELATION 21:1–2

Let us give close attention as the Bible describes not just a city, but the church, the bride of Christ:

> Then one of the seven angels…came to me and talked with me, saying, "Come, I will show you the bride, the Lamb's wife." And he carried me away in the Spirit to a great and high mountain, and showed me the great city, the holy Jerusalem, descending out of heaven from God, having the glory of God. Her light was like a most precious stone, like a jasper stone, clear as crystal.
>
> —REVELATION 21:9–11

Remember, the church is the bride of Christ, the Lamb:

2. In heaven, there will be "no more death, nor sorrow, nor crying. There shall be no more pain, for the former things have passed away" (Rev. 21:4).

3. Those who have received Jesus as their Savior will have a reserved place in heaven:

> Blessed be the God and Father of our Lord Jesus Christ, who according to His abundant mercy has begotten us again to a living hope through the resurrection of Jesus Christ from the dead, to an inheritance incorruptible and undefiled and that does not fade away, reserved in heaven for you.
>
> —1 PETER 1:3–4

4. In heaven, we will rule and reign with Christ:

> To him who overcomes I will grant to sit with Me on My throne, as I also overcame and sat down with My Father on His throne.
>
> —REVELATION 3:21

5. In heaven, we will worship and serve God:

Then the four living creatures said, "Amen!" And the twenty-four elders fell down and worshiped Him who lives forever and ever.

—Revelation 5:14

Therefore they [the redeemed] are before the throne of God, and serve Him day and night in His temple. And He who sits on the throne will dwell among them.

—Revelation 7:15

As we close this chapter, I want to thank God for the testimony and ministry of the apostles. They saw Jesus after His Resurrection, and they were not afraid to declare it. In fact, the Resurrection was one of the central themes of their ministry. They went out and preached Jesus to their generation, and multitudes were saved and received eternal life, escaping hell and eternal judgment.

Chapter 18

THE CHURCH

THE WORD *CHURCH* does not refer to a building, tabernacle, temple, or cathedral. The Greek language has a word, *kaleo*, which means, "I call." When we add a prefix to this word, it becomes *ek-kaleo*, meaning "I call out." The noun is *ecclesia*, meaning "the called-out ones." The church is "a group, an assembly, a fellowship of called-out people," called out of the natural world—called away from every conflicting philosophy—to follow Christ. The church is not the building. The church is the people who usually meet in buildings.

The word *church* was first used in the New Testament by Jesus Himself when He promised, "I will build my church; and the gates of hell shall not prevail against it" (Matt. 16:18, KJV). The word is used only one more time in the four Gospels. Jesus also described believers as "the kingdom of heaven" and "the kingdom of God." He saw these "called-out ones" manifesting a kingdom that would never fail.

We find the church more clearly defined and set forth in the Book of Acts and in the Epistles of Paul. The church is described in two important ways. Often the word is used to describe a "local body of believers"—a local church. At other times, it is obvious that the subject is "the whole church" or "the universal church."

In the local church examples, we read of "the church which was at Jerusalem" (Acts 8:1), "the church of God which is at Corinth" (1 Cor. 1:2), "the church of Ephesus" (Rev. 2:1); in Revelation 3, we read of "the church in Sardis," "the church in Philadelphia," and "the church of the Laodiceans."

JESUS: THE ONLY ENTRANCE TO THE CHURCH

The whole church is composed of all people—living and dead, past, present, and future—who receive God's salvation through Jesus Christ. Two great apostles, Peter and Paul, speaking to the religious people of their day, made it clear that Jesus is the only way to salvation:

> Let it be known to you all, and to all the people of Israel, that by the name of Jesus Christ of Nazareth, whom you crucified, whom God raised from the dead, by Him this man stands here before you whole. [This is the explanation of how a lame man was healed.] This is the "stone [Jesus] which was rejected by you builders, which has become the chief cornerstone." Nor is there salvation in any other, for there is no other name under heaven given among men by which we must be saved.
>
> —ACTS 4:10–12

> And He [God] put all things under His feet, and gave Him to be head over all things to the church, which is His body, the fullness of Him who fills all in all.
>
> —EPHESIANS 1:22–23

> But you have come to [this is present perfect tense—now, not future] Mount Zion and to the city of the living God, the heavenly Jerusalem, to an innumerable company of angels, to the general assembly and church of the firstborn [Jesus Christ] who are registered in heaven, to God the Judge of all, to the spirits of just men made perfect [justified men who are being perfected].
>
> —HEBREWS 12:22–23

All these terms—Mount Zion, the city of the living God, the heavenly Jerusalem, and the general assembly and church of the firstborn—are one and the same.

FAITH OF OUR FATHERS

Many people set out to find a list of church doctrines in the Bible. It is not there, but as we listen to (and read) the words of Jesus and the apostles, we begin to understand what is important to the church. The first and foremost thing is faith. The subject of the church is not introduced in the Bible until Peter makes his confession of faith in Jesus Christ:

> When Jesus came into the region of Caesarea Philippi, He asked His disciples, saying, "Who do men say that I, the Son of Man, am?" So they said, "Some say John the Baptist, some Elijah, and others Jeremiah or one of the prophets." He said to them, "But who do you say that I am?" Simon Peter answered and said, "You are the Christ, the Son of the living God." Jesus answered and said to him, "Blessed are you, Simon Bar-Jonah, for flesh and blood has not revealed this to you, but My Father who is in heaven. And I also say to you that you are Peter [Greek: small piece of stone], and on this rock [Greek: a mass of rock] I will build My church, and the gates of Hades shall not prevail against it."
> —MATTHEW 16:13–18

The general population, even the religious community, had much confusion about who Jesus was. But Peter had no confusion when he declared, "You are the Christ [Anointed One, Messiah], the Son of the living God." The important word here is not Peter (the small piece of stone), but the great revelation (faith confession) concerning Jesus.

At that moment, Jesus had found for Himself a "faith man," who, like Abraham in the Old Testament, was capable of receiving revelation from God. Building on Peter's faith confession, Jesus began to introduce the subject of His church. From that moment until the Second Coming of Jesus back to this earth, the only way anyone enters the church is by faith.

First, last, and always, the church is a body of believers. The church will have singers, workers, worshipers, and those who pray. These are the things they do. We can have a church that is weak in some of these areas (and that should not be), but there will never be a church without believers. Faith is the absolute, essential requirement of the church of the Lord Jesus Christ! In fact, "believers" and "those who believed" are sometimes used to refer to the church:

Now all who believed were together.

—ACTS 2:44

Now the multitude of those who believed were of one heart and one soul.

—ACTS 4:32

And believers were increasingly added to the Lord.

—ACTS 5:14

THE FELLOWSHIP

Just as faith is the entrance into the church, fellowship is the result of our being joined to the church. Paul makes this concept of fellowship very clear. To him, we Christians are members one of another because we are members in particular of the body of Christ.

If we are all in the same family with Jesus, the Christ—the Head—we are naturally in the same family with each other, as members of the body that belong to the Head. This means we are one body in Christ and members of one another. We collectively are the body of Christ and individually members of that body (Rom. 12:5; 1 Cor. 12:27).

In 1 Corinthians 1:9, we see the words *church* and *fellowship* merged together in a beautiful expression. Remember, church refers to those "called-out." Paul said, "God is faithful, by whom you were called into the fellowship (*koinonia*) of His Son, Jesus Christ our Lord." We are not only called out of this hopeless world system, but we are called into the glorious fellowship of Jesus, the Christ, the Son of God! The definition of this Greek word *koinonia* means "a partnership with participation, a communion."

It is possible to share a partnership that simply proves identity. But in the true church of Jesus Christ, we are not to have mere identity. We must participate. We must not be content with saying, "I belong to the church." We must say, "I belong to the church, and I'm active and involved in the church. I participate in the ministry of the church."

The Power of the Church Reaching
Out to the World

Jesus promised Peter that he would have the keys of the kingdom of heaven (Matt. 16:19). The purpose of keys is to open doors. On the Day of Pentecost, Peter used the keys. He preached the gospel of Jesus to the Jews and told them how to get into the church and the kingdom. Outstanding results followed his "door-opening ministry."

After Peter preached, those who heard him cried out, "What shall we do?" Peter's answer was clear and instantly given:

> Then Peter said to them, "Repent, and let every one of you be baptized in the name of Jesus Christ for the remission of sins; and you shall receive the gift of the Holy Spirit. For the promise is to you and to your children, and to all who are afar off, as many as the Lord our God will call"...Then those who gladly received his word were baptized; and that day about three thousand souls were added to them.
>
> —Acts 2:38–39, 41

Then, when he went to the house of Cornelius in Acts 10, he used the keys of the kingdom to open the door of the church to the Gentiles:

> Then Peter opened his mouth and said: "In truth I perceive that God shows no partiality. But in every nation whoever fears Him and works righteousness is accepted by Him. The word which God sent to the children of Israel, preaching peace through Jesus Christ—He is Lord of all—that word you know, which was proclaimed throughout all Judea, and began from Galilee after the baptism which John preached: how God anointed Jesus of Nazareth with the Holy Spirit and with power, who went about doing good and healing all who were oppressed by the devil, for God was with Him"....While Peter was still speaking these words, the Holy Spirit fell upon all those who heard the word. And those of the circumcision [Jewish brethren] who believed were astonished, as many as came with Peter, because the gift of the Holy Spirit had been poured out on the Gentiles also. For they heard them speak with tongues and magnify God.
>
> —Acts 10:34–38, 44–46

Before He ascended, Jesus had given a Great Commission to His disciples, telling them to go into all the world and "make disciples of all the nations" (Matt. 28:19). But when Peter was back in Jerusalem, many of the Jewish Christians were not too happy about these events. Peter gave them his testimony of what had happened to the Gentiles:

> And when there had been much dispute, Peter rose up and said to them: "Men and brethren, you know that a good while ago God chose among us, that by my mouth the Gentiles should hear the word of the gospel and believe." [This means they were believers and now part of the church.]
>
> —ACTS 15:7

After this meeting in Jerusalem, all of the apostles, including Paul and Barnabas, were released to go out with the gospel message to the whole world. It had taken a while for it to happen, but at last the divine intention of Jesus was being carried out, and the gospel God preached to Abraham was now being declared to the world, both Jew and Gentile. (See Galatians 3:8–9.)

Today, every minister and every believer has the authority to go out with the "gospel keys" to bring people into the kingdom of God and the church of the Lord Jesus Christ. The Bible gives a wealth of material describing the church. We have already established the fact that it is a "faith church" and that it is a fellowship of believers. But there is much more for us to learn about this "glorious church" (Eph. 5:27).

THE CHURCH IS CALLED THE BODY OF CHRIST

We cannot claim a relationship with Jesus as Head of the church without accepting the relationship we have with each other as members of the church, the body of Christ:

> So we, being many, are one body in Christ, and individually members of one another.
>
> —ROMANS 12:5

> Now you are the body of Christ, and members individually.
>
> —1 CORINTHIANS 12:27

[Paul is rejoicing in God's mighty power toward us who believe.] . . . which He worked in Christ when He raised Him from the dead and seated Him at His right hand in the heavenly places, far above all principality and power and might and dominion, and every name that is named, not only in this age but also in that which is to come. And He put all things under His feet, and gave Him to be head over all things to the church, which is His body, the fullness of Him who fills all in all.

—Ephesians 1:20–23

The Church Is Called the Bride of Christ

Paul, speaking to the Corinthian church, said, "For I am jealous for you with godly jealousy. For I have betrothed you to one husband, that I may present you as a chaste virgin to Christ" (2 Cor. 11:2):

Let us be glad and rejoice and give Him glory, for the marriage of the Lamb has come, and His wife has made herself ready. [Here Jesus is the Lamb; the wife is the church.]

—Revelation 19:7

Then I, John, saw the holy city, New Jerusalem, coming down out of heaven from God, prepared as a bride adorned for her husband.

—Revelation 21:2

The Church Is Called the Family of God

When we read over and over the scriptures about God being our Father, we are left with only one conclusion—we belong to the family of God. We have actually been adopted into His wonderful, glorious family:

But as many as received Him, to them He gave the right to become children of God, to those who believe in His name.

—John 1:12

I will be a Father to you, and you shall be My sons and daughters, says the Lord Almighty.

—2 Corinthians 6:18

And because you are sons, God has sent forth the Spirit of
His Son into your hearts, crying out, "Abba, [our very own]
Father!"

—GALATIANS 4:6

THE CHURCH IS CALLED GOD'S BUILDING, GOD'S HABITATION

We have stated that the building in which we meet is not the church; the
people are the church. It is these people who actually form a habitation, a
living place for God in this world. The original foundation of this building was laid by the apostles and prophets. Jesus Himself is declared to be
"the Chief Cornerstone":

Having been built on the foundation of the apostles and prophets,
Jesus Christ Himself being the chief cornerstone.

—EPHESIANS 2:20

For we are God's fellow workers; you are God's field, you are God's
building. According to the grace of God which was given to me,
as a wise master builder I have laid the foundation, and another
builds on it. But let each one take heed how he builds on it. For
no other foundation can anyone lay than that which is laid, which
is Jesus Christ.

—1 CORINTHIANS 3:9–11

Do you not know that you are the temple of God and that the
Spirit of God dwells in you?

—1 CORINTHIANS 3:16

WHAT ARE OUR RESPONSIBILITIES AS MEMBERS OF THIS GLORIOUS CHURCH?

After the Day of Pentecost and the outpouring of the Holy Spirit, the
believers undoubtedly asked themselves the question: Where do we go
from here? Once again, the Bible gives us the answer and tells us what
they began to do as they started their new church life:

And they continued steadfastly in the apostles' doctrine and fellowship, in the breaking of bread, and in prayers.

—ACTS 2:42

The first important word here is *continued*. This is one of the biggest problems we face in our church life. We often start with God in a fast run; after a few tests and pressures have come our way, we slow down and sometimes stop. Not these people! They started, they continued, they did not quit. They were faithful. They continued steadfastly in these important things:

- They continued *in the apostles' doctrine*—right doctrine. They didn't vote on what they believed. They had God-given leaders, and they were loyal to them. They respected them and followed them. The following words of Jesus tell us how He and the apostles evaluated their followers:

Then Jesus said to those Jews who believed Him, "If you abide [continue] in My word, you are My disciples indeed."

—JOHN 8:31

When the early church leaders had a problem with people leaving them, this was their attitude:

They went out from us, but they were not of us; for if they had been of us, they would have continued with us; but they went out that they might be made manifest, that none of them were of us...Therefore let that abide [continue] in you which you heard from the beginning. If what you heard from the beginning abides [continues] in you, you also will abide [continue] in the Son and in the Father.

—1 JOHN 2:19, 24

- They continued in *fellowship* with the Lord and with the members of the local assembly, the church. "All who believed were together...[they] were of one heart and one soul" (Acts 2:44, 4:32). Keep in mind what the word *fellowship* truly means—not only belonging, but also participating.

- They continued *in the breaking of bread (Communion)*. No place in the Bible describes Communion—the Lord's Supper—any more beautifully than Paul's words to the Corinthians:

> For I received from the Lord that which I also delivered to you: that the Lord Jesus on the same night in which He was betrayed took bread; and when He had given thanks, He broke it and said, "Take, eat; this is My body which is broken for you; do this in remembrance of Me." In the same manner He also took the cup after supper, saying, "This cup is the new covenant in My blood. This do, as often as you drink it, in remembrance of Me."
>
> —1 CORINTHIANS 11:23–25

- They continued *in prayers*. In five of Paul's letters to churches, he said, "I am making mention of you in my prayers." First Thessalonians 5:17 says we are to "pray without ceasing." We are to constantly be in an attitude of prayer:

> And whatever things you ask in prayer, believing, you will receive.
>
> —MATTHEW 21:22

THE MISSION OF THE CHURCH ON THIS EARTH

Jesus did not leave any doubt as to the mission of His church. We are to go into all the world and preach the gospel (Matt. 28:19). Through the ministry of apostles, prophets, evangelists, pastors, and teachers, the people of the church are to be trained to do the work of ministry. This involves every member of the church, not just full-time Christian workers. Only by bringing all the saints of God to a place of maturity can the job of evangelism really be done:

> And He Himself gave some to be apostles, some prophets, some evangelists, and some pastors and teachers, for the equipping of the saints for the work of ministry, for the edifying of the body of Christ.
>
> —EPHESIANS 4:11–12

In His final words to the apostles just before He went away, the Lord gave to them, and to His church this powerful challenge:

But you shall receive power when the Holy Spirit has come upon you; and you shall be witnesses to Me in Jerusalem, and in all Judea and Samaria, and to the end of the earth.

—ACTS 1:8

FINAL WORD: WHAT ABOUT THE MEETING PLACE?

We need to come together with the whole assembly often. This is a time of great celebration! We also need to meet together with small groups—in our homes, offices, working places, in restaurants—to share the joy of eating and fellowshiping together. In these small meetings, we can watch over each other and encourage and exhort each other.

This is needed, but there is also a warning in this area. Some people believe they are to meet with only a few people in the home. They reject apostolic and pastoral leadership and are likely to have a small vision and end up in error and unscriptural practices. For others, the television becomes their church.

This leads to spiritual anarchy and brings much confusion. We should have a central meeting place for the following reasons:

1. To have a strong witness in bringing the gospel to our community.

2. To develop spiritual unity among the whole local church in promoting God's programs.

3. To recognize the value of and submit to the teaching of the fivefold ministry, especially recognizing the authority of the apostolic and pastoral leadership in the church.

4. To experience the wonder, refreshing, excitement, strength, and celebration of powerful singing, praise, worship, and prayers of faith in the hour of our needs.

5. Most importantly, to influence our children and grandchildren in the habits, disciplines, and experiences of Christian living, unselfish cooperation, and sweet communion.

One final important word: What are you to do if you find yourself in a local church where there is confusion and no life, a place where the Word is not being preached and where you are not being fed? You should begin to ask God to lead you to a church where:

1. There is credible leadership, a leadership with a "track record" of integrity.

2. The leadership leads but does not manipulate and practice control over the people.

3. The Bible is esteemed as the authoritative Word of God.

4. The people believe in and practice the power and miraculous ministry of the Holy Spirit.

Chapter 19

THE MINISTRIES
AND
SPIRITUAL GIFTS

NOW THAT WE have learned about the beginning of the church, it is time to ask these important questions: How is it going to continue and succeed? Since Jesus has ascended to the throne, who is going to run the body of Christ, the church?"

It is easy to answer some of these questions. In the beginning, Jesus called "twelve, that they might be with Him" (Mark 3:14). He chose twelve apostles, to whom I refer as "the apostles of the Lamb." But that certainly cannot be the total answer for the leadership of the church. Those Twelve were not going to live forever, and someone else would have to be raised up to furnish leadership.

The first thing to be faced is that the physical presence of Jesus is gone! However, they were not fearful. In only a few days Jesus poured out the Holy Spirit upon His followers, and nothing was ever the same after that. Before the Acts 2 outpouring on the Day of Pentecost, God had been with His people; now He was dwelling in His people. This Holy Spirit is the source of many wonderful gifts that empower the church and bring great blessing to the people. But before we begin to study about these wonderful gifts of the Spirit, we want to introduce the great "secret weapon" of our Lord Jesus.

THE GIFT OF JESUS: THE ASCENSION GIFT MINISTRIES

After Jesus ascended to heaven, He began to call a new category of ministries into existence. We call these the fivefold ministry gifts and the ascension gift ministries. The following scripture is one of the most important to the future of the new covenant church:

> When He [Jesus] ascended on high, He led captivity captive, and gave gifts to men...and He Himself gave some to be apostles, some prophets, some evangelists, and some pastors and teachers, for the equipping of the saints for the work of ministry, for the edifying of the body of Christ.
> —EPHESIANS 4:8, 11–12

Notice the first word in this scripture passage—the word *when*. This denotes the time these ministries came into existence. When Jesus was in His earthly ministry, He called the twelve apostles. One of these, Judas Iscariot, became a traitor while Jesus was still alive. Judas lost his place as an apostle, not because he died, but because he could no longer perform the functions of the ministry, to be a witness of the death, burial, and Resurrection of the Lord Jesus Christ. There is no other successor to any of the Twelve. No one succeeded James. No one succeeded John, and no one succeeded the apostle Peter.

The Bible does not say one word about a successor to any of the Twelve. Paul was not one of the Twelve. They were "judicial witnesses" who were with Jesus from the baptism of John to the time He ascended into heaven (Acts 1:21–22.). There were, and are, many apostles, but the Twelve had no successors.[1]

---

[1] Some might object to this statement, because Matthias succeeded Judas. However, though Judas was one of the Twelve, he lost his apostleship because of his defection and traitorous conduct while still alive. The words in this prayer of Jesus tell the story: "While I was with them in the world, I kept them in Your name. Those whom You gave me I have kept; and none of them is lost except the son of perdition [the one headed for destruction], that the

The gift of these new ministries to the church was no mystery. Their purpose is plainly stated. They were to equip the saints (the members of the church) so they (the people) could do the work of the ministry. God's plan is glorious. The work of ministry is not to be carried on by a few professional people of the clergy. Everyone is not one of the fivefold ministries, but everyone in God's church does have a ministry. It is the responsibility of the apostles, prophets, evangelists, pastors, and teachers to prepare, train, and thus equip the people for their work of ministry in the church, the body of Christ. That is why it is so important to be a part of a good, strong Bible church. With the help of God's Word and the teaching and guidance of faithful ministers, we can do three things:

1. We can find our place of service and ministry in the body of Christ.

2. We can be trained for ministry and fill that place.

3. We can find direction and be given opportunity to function in our ministry.

The continuing purpose of these gifts is summed up in Ephesians 4:13–16. I give you my personal translation here. I think you will find it faithful to God's Word:

> These ministry gifts are to be in operation until we all come to the unity of the faith and of the knowledge of the Son of God, to a perfect, mature man [church], until we as the church come to the full stature and likeness of Christ. We should no longer be children, tossed one way and then the other, carried about with every wind of doctrine, influenced and tricked by false

---

Scripture might be fulfilled" (John 17:12).

The reference is to the prophecy in Psalm 109:8:

> Let his days be few, and let another take his office.

When the apostles gathered to select the one who would take Judas' place, they referred to this prophecy:

> For it is written in the book of Psalms: "Let his dwelling place be desolate, and let no one live in it" and "Let another take his office."
>
> —Acts 1:20

Two men who met the requirement of having been witnesses of Jesus from John's

teachers in their cunning craftiness and their deceitful plotting. Instead, we must speak the truth in love and grow up in Christ, under the authority of His headship. When this happens, the whole body of Christ will be joined and knit together by the contribution of what every member supplies. Then, when we are all doing "our share," the church will grow and be built up in love.

APOSTLES AND PROPHETS

Many religious groups readily accept the ministries of evangelists, pastors, and teachers, but they reject the present-day ministry of apostles and prophets. The word apostle(s) is used about eighty times in the New Testament. It means, "one sent forth, a messenger." The mission of the apostle was and is to establish churches and to be a father and an overseer to other ministries and churches. In Acts 14:4 and 14, Paul and Barnabas are referred to as apostles. In Romans 16:7, Andronicus and Junia are called apostles. None of these was part of the Twelve apostles of the Lamb called by Jesus to be with Him in His earthly ministry.

The word prophet(s) is used approximately sixty-eight times in the New Testament. Acts 13:1 says there were prophets in the local church at Antioch in Syria. Judas and Silas are called prophets in Acts 15:32, and Agabus is recognized as a prophet in Acts 21:10. Paul also states in 1 Corinthians 12:28 that prophets were appointed by God in the church.

We know these ministries are still in existence in the church today because their purpose, as stated in Ephesians 4:13–16, has not yet been fulfilled. We have not yet come "to the unity of the faith and of the knowledge of the Son of God, to a perfect man, to the measure of the stature of the fullness of Christ." Therefore, we know these ministries of apostles, prophets, evangelists, pastors, and teachers are still vitally needed.

---

baptism until the resurrection were set before them. They chose Matthias.

All of this occurred before Jesus gave the ascension gift ministries, beginning on the Day of Pentecost. When the Holy Spirit was poured out, the twelve "judicial witnesses" were already in place. There is no other commandment or any reason to appoint successors to the Twelve. Since the Day of Pentecost, all other apostles are "ascension gift apostles." This apostolic ministry is still valid in the church today.

A prophet speaks on behalf of God. His ministry is both forthtelling (prophetic preaching) and foretelling. He brings the revelation of the mind of God to the people and often reveals facts that could not be known by human knowledge. Here are some good Bible examples:

> And in these days prophets came from Jerusalem to Antioch. Then one of them, [there were more] named Agabus, stood up and showed by the Spirit that there was going to be a great famine throughout all the world, which also happened in the days of Claudius Caesar.
>
> —ACTS 11:27–28

> [Paul testifies]…by revelation He [God] made known to me the mystery (as I have briefly written already…) which in other ages was not made known to the sons of men, as it has now been revealed by the Spirit to His holy apostles and prophets.
>
> —EPHESIANS 3:3, 5

In addition to "revelation prophecies," the prophet can also speak words of "edification and exhortation and comfort" to the church (1 Cor. 14:3).

EVANGELISTS, PASTORS, AND TEACHERS

The evangelist can be a separate ministry, but it is often combined with other ministries. The evangelist is charged with the responsibility of proclaiming the "good news" of the gospel, bringing people to salvation. The New Testament evangelist can also be involved in planting churches and laying a biblical foundation for the lives of God's people. Paul's words to Timothy show us how versatile the evangelistic ministry can be:

> Preach the word! Be ready in season and out of season. Convince, rebuke, exhort, with all longsuffering and teaching…But you be watchful in all things, endure afflictions, do the work of an evangelist, fulfill your ministry.
>
> —2 TIMOTHY 4:2, 5

Another name used to describe the pastor is the word *shepherd*. His ministry is to care for the local church flock through preaching, counseling, correcting, admonishing (warning), teaching, and bringing compassionate discipline. The pastor should be supported by the church so he can give full time to his ministry, his "flock":

> Obey those who rule over you, and be submissive, for they watch out for your souls, as those who must give account. Let them do so with joy and not with grief, for that would be unprofitable for you.
> —HEBREWS 13:17

> Therefore take heed to yourselves and to all the flock, among which the Holy Spirit has made you overseers, to shepherd the church of God which He purchased with His own blood.
> —ACTS 20:28

> Do you not know that those who minister the holy things eat of the things of the temple, and those who serve at the altar partake of the offerings of the altar? Even so the Lord has commanded that those who preach the gospel should live from the gospel.
> —1 CORINTHIANS 9:13–14

> Let the elders who rule well be counted worthy of double honor, especially those who labor in the word and doctrine. For the Scripture says, "You shall not muzzle an ox while it treads out the grain," and, "The laborer is worthy of his wages."
> —1 TIMOTHY 5:17–18

The teacher, like the evangelist, can be a separate ministry, or it can be combined with other ministries. The teacher can serve in one home base or in a traveling ministry:

> Now in the church that was at Antioch there were certain prophets and teachers.
> —ACTS 13:1

> [Paul speaking]...I was appointed a preacher and an apostle—I am speaking the truth in Christ and not lying—a teacher of the Gentiles in faith and truth.
> —1 TIMOTHY 2:7

WHAT ABOUT ELDERS AND DEACONS?

The ministries of elders and deacons usually assist in the local church functions and needs. All of the five ministry gifts are elders, but there are also local church elders who are mature individuals, recognized as spiritual overseers in the local assembly. We believe elders should be able to teach and assist in caring for the needs of the people in ways such as serving Communion, anointing the sick, and declaring the Word of God:

> Is anyone among you sick? Let him call for the elders of the church, and let them pray over him, anointing him with oil in the name of the Lord.
>
> —JAMES 5:14

The meaning of the word *deacon* is "to serve or to minister." Deacons are ministers of "helps." They usually deal with individual assignments in the church, but they should live godly lives and be able to serve in spiritual capacities as well:

> And God has appointed these in the church: first apostles, second prophets, third teachers, after that miracles, then gifts of healings, helps, administrations, varieties of tongues.
>
> —1 CORINTHIANS 12:28

> Likewise deacons must be reverent, not double-tongued, not given to much wine, not greedy for money.
>
> —1 TIMOTHY 3:8

Women such as Phoebe served as deacons in the New Testament church (Rom. 16:1–2). We believe women can serve in any church capacity to which God has called them. Paul, following a Jewish ordinance, forbids women to teach or even ask questions in the open assembly. However, Scripture is overwhelming in the support of women having a place in the ministry. Even Paul declares that "in Christ [and therefore His church] there is to be no distinction between male and female":

> And it shall come to pass afterward that I will pour out My Spirit on all flesh; your sons and your daughters shall prophesy.
>
> —JOEL 2:28

There is neither Jew nor Greek [Gentile], there is neither slave nor free, there is neither male nor female; for you are all one in Christ Jesus.

—GALATIANS 3:28

THE GIFTS AND MANIFESTATIONS OF THE HOLY SPIRIT

The Holy Spirit can deal with the people of God in an infinite variety of ways. He is sovereign and can use God's people in any way He chooses. Nevertheless, Paul, writing to the church at Corinth, gives us a list of nine spiritual gifts:

> But the manifestation of the Spirit is given to each one for the profit of all: for to one is given the word of wisdom through the Spirit, to another the word of knowledge through the same Spirit, to another faith by the same Spirit, to another gifts of healings by the same Spirit, to another the working of miracles, to another prophecy, to another discerning of spirits, to another different kinds of tongues, to another the interpretation of tongues. But one and the same Spirit works all these things, distributing to each one individually as He wills.
>
> —1 CORINTHIANS 12:7–11

For clarity, we divide these nine gifts into three categories:

1. *Gifts of revelation*: Word of wisdom, word of knowledge, and the discerning of spirits.

2. *Gifts of power*: Faith, healing, and miracles.

3. *Gifts of utterance*: Prophecy, tongues, and interpretation of tongues.

Let me point out some important things about these gifts. It is not enough to merely believe these gifts are available. The Bible says, "the manifestation" is given to us. These gifts must "work" in the church. These gifts are given by the Holy Spirit, but all gifts are not given to each person. This is where the body ministry of the church is manifested. All are not apostles, and all do not have the same gifts. But when the whole church comes together, there are apostles, prophets, evangelists, pastors, and teachers. In the same sense, when the members of the body come together with their individual gifts, the church has a complete complement of ministry and gifts.

The answer to the following seven questions is no.

> Are all apostles? Are all prophets? Are all teachers? Are all workers of miracles? Do all have gifts of healings? Do all speak with tongues? Do all interpret?
>
> —1 Corinthians 12:29–30

We often hear questions like these: What is the value of these gifts? Should I desire to have them in my life? How could I receive them? The Bible is clear on these points. Paul says we should "earnestly desire" these gifts (1 Cor. 12:31, 14:1). These gifts are needed to build up and establish the church. They are needed to meet the spiritual and physical needs of God's people:

> A spiritual gift is given to each of us as a means of meeting the needs of the whole church.
>
> —1 Corinthians 12:7, author's paraphrase

> Even so you, since you are zealous for spiritual gifts, let it be for the edification of the church that you seek to excel.
>
> —1 Corinthians 14:12

Finally, how shall we receive these gifts? My answer: there is no one set way of receiving spiritual gifts into our lives. God is sovereign, and He can do what He wants to do in any way He wants to do it. Consider the following statements:

1. Spiritual gifts can be received as the result of our own prayers to God.

2. A sovereign manifestation can come to us when we receive an infilling of the Holy Spirit. When Paul laid hands on the believers at Ephesus, "they spoke with tongues and prophesied" (Acts 19:6).

3. Gifts of the Holy Spirit can be imparted by the laying-on of the hands of the presbytery with prophecy:

Do not neglect the gift that is in you, which was given to you by prophecy with the laying on of the hands of the eldership [presbytery].

—1 TIMOTHY 4:14

Chapter 20

The Lord's Supper

In the New Testament, we read about the Lord's Supper, also called Communion. I want to define these terms and explain what they mean to us, but this would be the wrong place to begin. To correctly understand what the Lord's Supper is all about, we must begin in the Old Testament, not the New.

When it was time for the people of Israel to come out of their Egyptian bondage, God instituted a most unusual event, called the Passover. In Egypt, the people of Israel lived in slavery, and the boy babies were killed. Now, it was time for God to deliver His people, and in the process of this deliverance, He was going to bring great judgment upon the Egyptians. A death angel was to pass through the land and kill all of the firstborn of the Egyptians. Here is the way God planned it:

The Beginning of the "Passover"

Now the Lord spoke to Moses and Aaron in the land of Egypt, saying… "Speak to all the congregation of Israel, saying: 'On the tenth of this month every man shall take for himself a lamb, according to the house of his father, a lamb for a household… Your lamb shall be without blemish, a male of the first year. You may take it from the sheep or from the goats. Now you shall keep it until the fourteenth day of the same month. Then the whole assembly of the congregation of Israel shall kill it at twilight. And they shall take some of the blood and put it on the two doorposts and on the lintel of the houses where they eat it . . . And thus you shall eat it: with a belt on your waist, your sandals on your feet, and your staff in your hand. So you shall eat it in haste. It is the Lord's Passover. For I will pass through the land of Egypt on that night, and will strike all the firstborn in the land of Egypt, both man and beast; and against all the gods of Egypt I will execute judgment: I am the Lord. Now the blood shall be a sign for you on the houses where you are. And when I see the blood, I will pass over you; and the plague shall not be on you to destroy you when I strike the land of Egypt. So this day shall be to you a memorial; and you shall keep it as a feast to the Lord throughout your generations."

—EXODUS 12:1, 3, 5–7, 11–14

We get the term Passover from the promise that the death angel would pass (skip) over every house where the blood was placed on the doorposts. Down through the years, the people of Israel continued to celebrate this Passover, remembering the time God had brought them out of Egypt. But they did not understand that all of this was a "type" and a "shadow" of the true Passover Lamb who was to come. All of the lambs killed under the old covenant could never deliver God's people from the bondage of sin. But when Jesus came on the scene, everything changed:

For if the blood of bulls and goats and the ashes of a heifer, sprinkling the unclean, sanctifies for the purifying of the flesh, how much more shall the blood of Christ, who through the eternal Spirit offered Himself without spot to God, cleanse your conscience from dead works to serve the living God? And for this reason He is the Mediator of the new covenant, by means of death, for the redemption of the transgressions under the first covenant, that those who are called may receive the promise of the eternal inheritance.

—HEBREWS 9:13–15

> For it is not possible that the blood of bulls and goats could take
> away sins.
>
> —Hebrews 10:4

The Announcement of the Lamb of God

John the Baptist was preaching and baptizing by the Jordan River. One day, he saw Jesus walking toward him and cried out, "Behold! The Lamb of God who takes away the sin of the world!" (John 1:29). Paul also understood that Jesus was the Passover Lamb. He told the Corinthian church, "For indeed Christ, our Passover, was sacrificed for us" (1 Cor. 5:7).

Toward the end of His earthly ministry, Jesus knew it was time for Him to fulfill the Word of God and bring reality to the Passover experience. The story of what happened when Jesus met with His disciples for the Passover is beautifully told in Matthew 26:1–2, 26–28, and Luke 22:14–20.

Nevertheless, my favorite telling of the Passover story is given by Paul the Apostle. He received a marvelous revelation of what happened on that night and tells it to the church in Corinth. This speaks about the last night before the cross:

> For I received from the Lord that which I also delivered to you: that the Lord Jesus on the same night in which He was betrayed took bread; and when He had given thanks, He broke it and said, "Take, eat; this is My body which is broken for you; do this in remembrance of Me." In the same manner He also took the cup after supper, saying, "This cup is the new covenant in My blood. This do, as often as you drink it, in remembrance of Me." For as often as you eat this bread and drink this cup, you proclaim [show, declare, and teach] the Lord's death till He comes. Therefore whoever eats this bread or drinks this cup of the Lord in an unworthy manner will be guilty of the body and blood of the Lord. But let a man examine himself, and so let him eat of the bread and drink of the cup. For he who eats and drinks in an unworthy manner eats and drinks judgment to himself, not discerning [not properly appreciating the value of] the Lord's body. For this reason many are weak [feeble before their time] and sick among you, and many sleep [to be put to sleep, die]. For if we would judge ourselves, we would not be judged.
>
> —1 Corinthians 11:23–31

THE DEATH OF THE LAMB

They finished the Passover celebration, left the room, and within twenty-four hours, Jesus had become the true Passover Lamb by dying on the cross. All the blood of the animals in the old covenant could never take away our sins, but the blood of Jesus did. Jesus made this clear when He was with His disciples. "For this is My blood of the new covenant, which is shed for many for the remission of sins" (Matt. 26:28). John 19:14 tells us Jesus died on "the Preparation Day of the Passover."

DIFFERENT NAMES FOR THE COMMUNION EXPERIENCE

When we come together and share the bread and the cup, we are obeying the words of our Lord. Here are different Bible names for this experience. It is called:

- "The breaking of bread" (Acts 2:42, 20:7)

- "The Lord's Supper" (1 Cor. 11:20)

- "Communion" (1 Cor. 10:16–17)

> The cup of blessing which we bless, is it not the communion of the blood of Christ? The bread which we break, is it not the communion of the body of Christ? For we, though many, are one bread and one body; for we all partake of that one bread.
> —1 CORINTHIANS 10:16–17

The word *communion* in the Greek language is *koinonia*, meaning, "a partnership, a participation, a communion and a fellowship." Communion is not a sad time. Jesus died on the cross and became sin for us, shedding His precious blood that we might have the remission (forgiveness) of all our sins. Then came the Resurrection and His ascension into heaven, where He sits on His kingly throne. This is a story with a happy ending!

Our participation in Communion should be a time for rejoicing, a time of fellowship and thanksgiving to God for providing such a marvelous plan for us. It should also be a time of fellowship, thanksgiving, and praise with the body of Christ. It is a time to make certain we are living a clean life and walking in obedience to God's Word. It is also the time to make certain no bitterness, resentment, jealousy, or unforgiving spirit comes between us and our brothers and sisters in Christ.

Remember, we have no choice in the matter. Jesus has deliberately put Communion in front of us. We must do it on a regular basis, and we must do it with a clean heart and a forgiving spirit. If we partake of Communion with an unholy attitude or any kind of resentment or unforgiving attitude, we put poison into the body of Christ and eat and drink "judgment" to ourselves (1 Cor. 11:29). However, we also sin if we refuse Communion because our life is not right. It is the sin of rebellion against the Word of God.

What we should do is this: ask God to forgive us and cleanse our hearts and then eat in faith with rejoicing!

JESUS DEMONSTRATES THE COMMUNION ORDER

In the Matthew account, we see the beautiful pattern set forth for Communion. Here is the way it is revealed:

> As they were eating, Jesus took bread, blessed and broke it, and gave it to the disciples and said, "Take, eat... Then He took the cup, and gave thanks, and gave it to them saying, "Drink from it all of you. For this is My blood of the new covenant."
> —MATTHEW 26:26–28

WE ALSO SEE THE COMMUNION DRAMA ACTED OUT IN THE LIFE OF JESUS

In His earthly ministry, Jesus clearly stated, "I am the bread of life" (John 6:35). On two dramatic occasions, He uses the same "divine order" that we see in Communion:

- At the feeding of the five thousand. (This is the only miracle of Jesus that is reported in all four Gospels.):

> Then He commanded the multitudes to sit down on the grass. And He took the five loaves and the two fish, and looking up to heaven, He blessed and broke and gave the loaves to the disciples; and the disciples gave to the multitudes. So they all ate and were

filled, and they took up twelve baskets full of the fragments that remained.

—MATTHEW 14:19–20

- After His Resurrection, Jesus revealed Himself to two of His disciples in a most unusual way:

Now it came to pass, as He sat at the table with them, that He took bread, blessed and broke it, and gave it to them. Then their eyes were opened and they knew Him; and He vanished from their sight.

—LUKE 24:30–31

The main thing about Communion is that we are remembering the death of Jesus on the cross and what He purchased for us. In addition, it demonstrates the fellowship we have with the Lord Jesus and with every other member of the body of Christ. As we eat the bread, we are remembering His broken body; as we drink the "fruit of the vine" (Matt. 26:29), we are remembering His shed blood that brings salvation, redemption, and eternal life to us.

Jesus was a glorious gift from God, and this experience of Communion is a wonderful gift from Jesus to His church!

Chapter 21

The Joy of Belonging

Loneliness is one of the most awful feelings in the world. Grown, mature, highly intelligent, and, sometimes wealthy, men and women join unusual clubs with strange rules and regulations because they do not want to be alone. They may dress in unbelievable costumes, agree to restrictive codes of conduct, and practice secret hand-shakes, all because they want to "belong." Although I do not belong to such a group, I can understand the motives of those who do. I am so delighted that I have found a greater, more wonderful answer—a godly plan that will bring great joy to our lives. It is the joy of belonging to things that God has blessed.

Part I: The Joy of the Family

When I hear the word *family*, I get a warm feeling. I was reared in a Christian home by godly parents. My wife had the same experience. Both of our children married into godly homes, and so the joy continues.

Before there was a nation of Israel, before there was a church, there was a man and a woman with a love relationship invented by God. The man's name was Adam, and God saw he needed someone in his life to keep him from being alone. God performed a miraculous operation, and from the man He took a rib and created a woman, whom Adam called Eve.

From this man and woman, God brought forth children, grandchildren, and a whole human family. It is God's plan and will that this family relationship will offer companionship, create success in our lives, offer hope for every tomorrow, and produce faith and love to solve problems and meet our needs.

The correct beginning for every family is for a godly man to marry a godly woman. This marriage is to be a covenant union between the two people, to be dissolved only by the death of one of the parties. Jesus said, "They are no longer two but one flesh. Therefore what God has joined together, let not man separate" (Matt. 19:6).

This marriage relationship is an earthly drama representing the spiritual and heavenly union of Christ and the church; the husband plays the role of Christ, and the wife plays the role of the church. When you read God's Word, it is easy to see the kind of relationship and the love that should be manifested in every marriage:

> For the husband is head of the wife, as also Christ is head of the church; and He is the Savior of the body. Therefore, just as the church is subject to Christ, so let the wives be to their own husbands in everything. Husbands, love your wives, just as Christ also loved the church and gave Himself for her.
>
> —EPHESIANS 5:23–25

In the old and new covenants, God warns the godly not to marry the ungodly:

> Nor shall you make marriages with them [the ungodly]. You shall not give your daughter to their son, nor take their daughter for your son. For they will turn your sons away from following Me, to serve other gods; so the anger of the LORD will be aroused against you and destroy you suddenly.
>
> —DEUTERONOMY 7:3–4

> Do not be unequally yoked together with unbelievers. For what fellowship has righteousness with lawlessness? And what communion has light with darkness?
>
> —2 CORINTHIANS 6:14

If you are thinking of going into a new business, you might want to consider this scripture when you choose your business partners.

HUSBANDS, WIVES, AND CHILDREN

Everyone in the family should share in the joy of the family, but everyone also has responsibilities in the family unit. In the home, husbands (and fathers) have the greatest responsibility in the sight of God. In Ephesians 5:22–25, Paul gives some very difficult assignments to the husband and the wife. He says the husband must love his wife in the same way Christ loved the church and gave himself for her. He says the wife should submit herself to her husband "as to the Lord," in the same way the church submits to her Lord.

The question must be asked: Will this work in today's society? I believe it will, and the key is primarily in the hands of the husband. If he will love his wife in the same way Christ loved (and loves) the church, the wife's submission will not be a harsh thing, but a joy.

I have seen some "hardheaded" and selfish men treat their wives with contempt, arrogance, insensitivity, and even physical abuse—and still expect them to graciously submit. This is foolish. (There are exceptions, but when a man is properly submitted to God, the wife will not find it difficult to submit to the husband.) A good husband should protect his wife, provide for her, and be the priest of the home. The wife should be the joy of her husband and work with him. She should pray for him and be his number one encourager in their life together.

What happens if either the husband or wife comes to God and the other partner does not? The answer is simple. The "saved" partner should live and love in such a way that the other one would want to come to Jesus. Sometimes, this does not happen at once, but we should keep on praying and believing it will happen.

This was one man's testimony: "My wife got saved and started going to church. At first, I thought she was crazy. Then, I noticed that things began to work better in our house. She began to express her love for me in a more exciting way than I had ever known. I figured I had better check this church out. The first time I went with her, I answered the invitation and gave my heart to the Lord."

The Word of God does not allow us to divorce our husband or wife just because they are unsaved and do not go to church. First Peter 3:1 tells us that an ungodly husband can be won to the Lord by the godly life of a wife. This godly attitude will speak louder than any harsh words.

What About the Responsibilities of Parents and Children?

Just as God is responsible for His creation, husbands and wives are also responsible for their creation—their children. Parents should not only love their children, but they should also express that love by word and deed. Children feel secure when they know they are loved.

Soon after children are born or soon after parents come to God, the parents should bring their babies and children to the church and dedicate them to the Lord before the whole congregation. Shortly after the birth of Jesus, Mary and Joseph brought Jesus to Jerusalem "to present Him to the Lord." (Luke 2:22). This is a marvelous example for us to follow.

Parents Have a Continuing Duty to Their Children

1. They should teach them and train them in the ways of God:

You shall teach them [the commandments and the Word of God] diligently to your children, and shall talk of them when you sit in your house, when you walk by the way, when you lie down, and when you rise up.

—Deuteronomy 6:7

Train up a child in the way he should go, and when he is old he will not depart from it.

—Proverbs 22:6

2. They should provide for them:

For the children ought not to lay up for the parents, but the parents for the children.

—2 Corinthians 12:14

3. They should love and correct them, setting a godly example for them to follow:

For whom the Lord loves He corrects, just as a father the son in whom he delights.

—Proverbs 3:12

Chasten your son while there is hope, and do not set your heart on his destruction.

—Proverbs 19:18

Foolishness is bound up in the heart of a child; the rod of correction will drive it far from him.

—Proverbs 22:15

The purpose of discipline is to break the stubborn will, but do not degrade your child or discipline in anger. Most good teachers will tell you to attack the problem, not the person.

Children Have a Responsibility to Their Parents

1. They should honor and obey their parents:

A wise son makes a glad father, but a foolish son is the grief of his mother.

—Proverbs 10:1

Children, obey your parents in the Lord, for this is right. "Honor your father and mother," which is the first commandment with promise: "that it may be well with you and you may live long on the earth."

—Ephesians 6:1–3

2. They should honor and serve God, and they should be involved in church life. There is no certain "age of accountability." When children feel their need and come under the conviction of the Holy Spirit, they should be encouraged to surrender their lives to God:

Now all Judah, with their little ones, their wives, and their children, stood before the Lord.

—2 Chronicles 20:13

But when the chief priests and scribes saw the wonderful things that He did, and the children crying out in the temple and saying, "Hosanna to the Son of David!" they were indignant.

—MATTHEW 21:15

The Bible gives us examples of children involved in godly things. It is no wonder the boy Samuel grew up to be such a mighty man of God. He was dedicated to the Lord as a baby and grew up in the home of the high priest (1 Sam. 2:18). A mere "lad" gave his lunch to Jesus, resulting in the miraculous feeding of the five thousand (John 6:9).

WHAT ABOUT DIVORCE?

This is a delicate subject, and before we go any further, I will tell you that God is not pleased with divorce! Nevertheless, with strong restrictions, God has allowed for the possibility of divorce, both in the Old and New Testaments. Sin causes separation between God and mankind, and sin is also the root cause of broken relationships between husbands and wives.

There are times when one marriage partner walks away from the marriage, and even an innocent party can do nothing about it. Paul addresses this situation:

But if the unbeliever departs, let him depart; a brother or a sister is not under bondage in such cases. But God has called us to peace.

—1 CORINTHIANS 7:15

In the old covenant, God was a husband to Israel. He made a covenant with them and promised He would be their God and they would be His people. The record reveals that the people of Israel were unfaithful to God. Over and over they committed spiritual adultery by going into idolatry like all the heathen nations around them. When this pattern of unfaithfulness became evident, God spoke to Israel through His prophet Jeremiah and told them He was going to make a new marriage covenant:

Behold, the days are coming, says the Lord, when I will make a new covenant with the house of Israel and with the house of Judah—not according to the covenant that I made with their fathers in the day that I took them by the hand to lead them out of the land of Egypt, My covenant which they broke, though I was a husband to them, says the Lord.

—JEREMIAH 31:31–32

Christians should do everything in their power to avoid divorce. In today's world, a man or woman often gives this excuse, "We were incompatible." These are foolish words. Every man and woman is incompatible. We are nothing alike. We are made differently, think differently, and feel different. Real love will help us overcome the incompatible things and enjoy the love part of marriage. If this relationship stays right and we practice respect toward each other, the differences will become, as it were, only a "bump in the road" of a joyful marriage.

Let us consider one more thing about love. It is not just a human emotion based on sexual attractiveness. It is actually an act of the will. When temptation comes, we have the ability to say no. We must not let our mind dwell with unholy desire upon some other woman or man. The Bible teaches that we have the power to control our thought process. We can set our affections and our mind on God, and we can do the same thing with our husband or wife. Paul says, "Set your mind [affection] on things above, not on things on the earth" (Col. 3:2).

This expression, affection or mind, is the Greek word *phroneo*. It means "to exercise the mind, set the affection on, be of one and the same." It will work with God, and it will work in your marriage.

Jesus, speaking on the subject of marriage and divorce, made this statement:

And I say to you, whoever divorces his wife, except for sexual immorality, and marries another, commits adultery; and whoever marries her who is divorced commits adultery.

—MATTHEW 19:9

Paul sums it up in these words:

Now to the married I command, yet not I but the Lord: A wife is not to depart from her husband. But even if she does depart, let her remain unmarried or be reconciled to her husband. And a husband is not to divorce his wife...But if the unbeliever departs, let him depart; a brother or a sister is not under bondage in such cases. But God has called us to peace.

—1 CORINTHIANS 7:10–11, 15

PART II: THE JOY OF GIVING

The Bible speaks of tithes and offerings. Our word *tithe* means "one tenth." (See Leviticus 27:32; Genesis 14:20; Hebrews 7:4.) The people of God were to bring to the priest one-tenth of all their increase. In addition, they were asked to bring offerings for special occasions. Many reject the idea of tithing because they say it was "under the Law." This is not true. The first time the word *tithe* is used in the Bible is in the life of Abraham. This was hundreds of years before the law was given on Mount Sinai.

Abraham had returned victorious from a great battle:

> Then Melchizedek king of Salem brought out bread and wine; he was the priest of God Most High. And he blessed him and said: "Blessed be Abram of God Most High, Possessor of heaven and earth; and blessed be God Most High, who has delivered your enemies into your hand." And he [Abraham] gave him [Melchizedek] a tithe of all.
>
> —GENESIS 14:18–20

It is our belief that Melchizedek was a pre-incarnate revelation of Jesus, the Christ. Read Hebrews 7:1–7 for more exciting information about Melchizedek.

Abraham's grandson Jacob asked for God's blessing and committed himself to tithe. He said, "Of all that You give me I will surely give a tenth to You" (Gen. 28:22). This was five hundred years before the Law.

When God did establish the Law with Israel, He continued the principle of tithing. In fact, the tithe was so important that if Israel wanted to borrow God's tithe and use it for some other purpose, He charged them an interest rate of 20 percent. It is wise to quickly separate God's tithe from all your other funds:

> And all the tithe of the land, whether of the seed of the land or of the fruit of the tree, is the Lord's. It is holy to the Lord. If a man wants at all to redeem any of his tithes, he shall add one-fifth to it.
>
> —LEVITICUS 27:30–31

Under the old covenant, the people were to bring their tithe to a certain place called the storehouse, in the custody of the Levites (priests, ministers of God). Under the new covenant, we are to bring our tithe to the local church. The Bible is very clear on this point:

> "Bring all the tithes into the storehouse, that there may be food in My house, and try Me now in this," Says the Lord of hosts, "If I will not open for you the windows of heaven and pour out for you such blessing that there will not be room enough to receive it."
>
> —MALACHI 3:10

> On the first day of the week [Sunday] let each one of you lay something aside, storing up as he may prosper, that there be no collections when I come.
>
> —1 CORINTHIANS 16:2

The purpose of the tithe is to support the ministry and to provide for the many functions and expenses of the local assembly. There will be an abundance of "meat-provisions" in God's house when all of His people pay their tithes to Him. "Even so the Lord has commanded that those who preach the gospel should live from the gospel" (1 Cor. 9:14).

Jesus put His stamp of approval upon the tithe. The scribes and Pharisees paid their tithe, but they neglected the matters of "justice and mercy and faith." Jesus said in Matthew 23:23, "These [the tithes] you ought to have done, without leaving the others undone."

Our use of money is often the "acid test" of our character, our relationship with God, and our faith in Him. It reveals the level on which we place God in our affairs. It is a revelation of our heart attitude. Remember, we do not give our tithe—we pay it. Leviticus 27:30 tells us "the tithe…is the Lord's." Whatever we have, it came from God. He is the source of all we own or possess. Deuteronomy 8:18 says, "And you shall remember the Lord your God, for it is He who gives you power to get wealth." God owns it all, and we are His stewards or caretakers.

People with no commitment and no faith often raise these two problems:

1. "I can't afford to tithe. I am too poor. I do not make enough money."

2. Some who are rich say, "You can't expect me to give that
   much to God!"

The problem is that we do not believe the Word of God. We lack faith.
We do not trust God:

> "Will a man rob God? Yet you have robbed Me! But you say, 'In
> what way have we robbed You?'" In tithes and offerings...Bring
> all the tithes into the storehouse, that there may be food in My
> house, and try Me now in this," [This is one place where God
> says we can test Him and His Word.] Says the Lord of hosts, "If
> I will not open for you the windows of heaven and pour out for
> you such blessing that there will not be room enough to receive
> it. And I will rebuke the devourer for your sakes, so that he will
> not destroy the fruit of your ground, nor shall the vine fail to bear
> fruit for you in the field," says the Lord of hosts.
>
> —MALACHI 3:8, 10–11

When we are tithers, God is fighting on our team. He is working on
our job, helping us run our business, sell our product, and watching over
everything in our possession. Otherwise we are in the struggle alone.

- Remember that God owns everything, and we are His stewards:

> For every beast of the forest is Mine, and the cattle on a thousand
> hills. I know all the birds of the mountains, and the wild beasts of
> the field are Mine. If I were hungry, I would not tell you; for the
> world is Mine, and all its fullness.
>
> —PSALM 50:10–12

- Jesus taught this attitude on giving money or any possession:

> Give, and it will be given to you: good measure, pressed down,
> shaken together, and running over will be put into your bosom.
> For with the same measure that you use, it will be measured back
> to you.
>
> —LUKE 6:38

- Here is Paul's admonition on giving:

So let each one give as he purposes in his heart, not grudgingly or of necessity; for God loves a cheerful giver.

—2 CORINTHIANS 9:7

PART 3: THE JOY OF CORRECTION AND RESTORATION

The church is not in the punishing business. We are in the restoration business. If people make a mistake, if they get sidetracked, we are here to help them. The government has the right to punish. The church is to teach, admonish, correct, and restore.

We must take the proper steps when people begin to live unclean lives, when they become disruptive in the house of God, when they abuse others, and when they rebel against the counsel of God's appointed leaders—apostles, prophets, evangelists, pastors, teachers, and elders. The following forms of discipline are available to the church:

1. Admonish (confront with the hope of restoring) and rebuke its members.

2. We may ask them not to eat at the Lord's table. This indicates we are not in fellowship with their misconduct.

3. Finally, with the agreement of the elders of the church, we have the right to exclude them from membership in the local assembly.

4. The church has no power (and should not desire that power) to excommunicate anyone from the forgiveness, grace, and mercy of God.

SOLVING PROBLEMS BETWEEN INDIVIDUALS

When there is a problem between individuals, Jesus instructs us in the way of restoration:

> Moreover if your brother sins against you, go and tell him his fault between you and him alone. If he hears you, you have gained your brother. But if he will not hear, take with you one or two more, that "by the mouth of two or three witnesses every word

may be established." And if he refuses to hear them, tell it to the church. But if he refuses even to hear the church, let him be to you like a heathen and a tax collector.

—MATTHEW 18:15–17

PAUL DEALS WITH ONE WHO HAS COMMITTED SEXUAL SINS

In the name of our Lord Jesus Christ, when you are gathered together, along with my spirit, with the power of our Lord Jesus Christ, deliver such a one to Satan for the destruction of the flesh, that his spirit may be saved in the day of the Lord Jesus...Do you not know that a little leaven leavens the whole lump?...But now I have written to you not to keep company with anyone named a brother, who is sexually immoral, or covetous, or an idolater, or a reviler, or a drunkard, or an extortioner—not even to eat with such a person...But those who are outside God judges. Therefore "put away from yourselves the evil person."

—1 CORINTHIANS 5:4–6, 11, 13

BIBLICAL RULES FOR CORRECTION OF ELDERS

Do not receive an accusation against an elder except from two or three witnesses. Those who are sinning rebuke in the presence of all, that the rest also may fear.

—1 TIMOTHY 5:19–20

In all correction, the objective must be restoration, if possible:

Brethren, if a man is overtaken in any trespass, you who are spiritual restore such a one in a spirit of gentleness, considering yourself lest you also be tempted. Bear one another's burdens, and so fulfill the law of Christ.

—GALATIANS 6:1–2

Chapter 22

PRAYER, PRAISE, AND WORSHIP

THESE THREE WORDS —prayer, praise, and worship—can be divided, but they are far more effective when they work together. Therefore, we will study them as one complete teaching in this lesson.

PART I: PRAYER

The first statement about prayer concerns our attitude toward God:

> But without faith it is impossible to please Him, for he who comes to God must believe that He is, and that He is a rewarder of those who diligently seek Him.
>
> —HEBREWS 11:6

Two basic things are stated here, and faith is involved in both. We must believe:

1. God really does exist.
2. He rewards those who diligently seek Him.

When many people think of prayer, they begin to make a list of what they want from God, and then they start talking. I define prayer in a most simple way: "Prayer is our communicating with God, and God with us." So prayer works in two directions: (1) We talk to God, (2) We listen for God to speak to us. Also, prayer is not always audible conversation. It can be silent—in our minds—and still be intense and effective.

Jesus did not try to argue the need for prayer. It was just something He did and told His followers to do. In His days on earth, He warned them not to stand on the streets and "pray for show." Today, there are many places where we are not allowed to pray publicly. Yet, there is still much prayer that is "window dressing," praying to be seen or heard. There is also much praying with "vain repetitions," which will accomplish little or nothing (Matt. 6:7).

The reason we mention Jesus and prayer together is important. If prayer was necessary in the life of Jesus, it certainly is needed in our lives. When we pray, we are exposed to four powerful opportunities:

1. To the words God wants to speak to us.

2. To direction from God and instructions concerning His will for our lives.

3. To the wonder and power of God's holy presence.

4. Our requests can be answered, our needs met.

It is now time for us to learn what Jesus said and taught about prayer. The following scripture verses contain what is commonly called "the Lord's Prayer." It probably should be known as "the disciples' prayer":

> And when you pray, you shall not be like the hypocrites. For they love to pray standing in the synagogues and on the corners of the streets, that they may be seen by men. Assuredly, I say to you, they have their reward. But you, when you pray, go into your room, and when you have shut your door, pray to your Father who is in the secret place; and your Father who sees in secret will reward you openly. And when you pray, do not use vain repetitions as the heathen do. For they think that they will be heard for their many words. Therefore do not be like them. For your Father

knows the things you have need of before you ask Him. In this manner, therefore, pray:

Our Father in heaven, hallowed be Your name. Your kingdom come. Your will be done on earth as it is in heaven. Give us this day our daily bread. And forgive us our debts, as we forgive our debtors. And do not lead us into temptation, but deliver us from the evil one. For Yours is the kingdom and the power and the glory forever. Amen.

—MATTHEW 6:5–13

Notice that Jesus did not say, "If you pray." Three times He said, "When you pray." He assumes that if we are His disciples, we will pray. I was once teaching a lesson on prayer, and I had told about various tests and trials through which I had come. A little lady almost one hundred years old raised her hand, requesting permission to speak. She spoke to me, but we knew it was God's word to all of us. She said, "Son, don't you think God will always leave us something in our lives to pray about?" We all laughed and answered with a loud, "Yes!"

The Lord's Prayer is not legalistic. Jesus did not tell us to pray these exact words, but "in this manner." Some have taught that this prayer was "under the Law" and does not apply to us, but this cannot be true. Jesus Himself plainly declared, "The law and the prophets were until John [the Baptist]. Since that time the kingdom of God has been preached, and everyone is pressing into it" (Luke 16:16). This was and is a kingdom prayer! It was for the Twelve and for us.

THE POWER IN BINDING, LOOSING, AND AGREEING

Jesus gave us more words on the powerful results of prayer in Matthew 18:18–20:

Assuredly, I say to you, whatever you bind on earth will be bound in heaven, and whatever you loose on earth will be loosed in heaven. Again I say to you that if two of you agree on earth concerning anything that they ask, it will be done for them by My Father in heaven. For where two or three are gathered together in My name, I am there in the midst of them.

In these words of Jesus, we learn some important facts. We are not at the mercy of circumstances or the power of the devil. We have the "power of agreement." It is obvious we are not to merely pray alone when problems arise, but we are to find another "faith person" who will believe what we believe and come into "faith agreement" with us. The result is that it will be done!

Let's not just talk about "agreeing." Let's do it. Join with "faith partners" in a Bible-believing, Spirit-filled local church, and make your petitions known to God.

- If you are sick, tell Him what is wrong and that you want to be made whole.

- If you have grown cold and need a refreshing of the fire of God, admit it.

- If you have failed or sinned, confess it and ask forgiveness.

Remember, we are not alone. Jesus is with us, and He is our High Priest, who can "be touched with the feeling of our infirmities… [because He] was in all points tempted like as we are, yet without sin" (Heb. 4:15, KJV).

ASK, BELIEVE, AND DO NOT GIVE UP!

One of the great lessons Jesus taught about prayer was perseverance. When we pray, we must never give up:

> Then He spoke a parable to them, that men always ought to pray and not lose heart, saying: "There was in a certain city a judge who did not fear God nor regard man. Now there was a widow in that city; and she came to him, saying, 'Get justice for me from my adversary.' And he would not for a while; but afterward he said within himself, 'Though I do not fear God nor regard man, yet because this widow troubles me I will avenge her, lest by her continual coming she weary me.'" Then the Lord said, "Hear what the unjust judge said. And shall God not avenge His own elect who cry out day and night to Him, though He bears long with them? I tell you that He will avenge them speedily."
> —LUKE 18:1–8

Jesus spoke these encouraging words to His disciples concerning prayer:

> So Jesus answered and said to them, "Have faith in God. For assuredly, I say to you, whoever [any believer] says to this mountain, 'Be removed and be cast into the sea,' and does not doubt in his heart, but believes that those things he says will be done, he will have whatever he says. Therefore I say to you, whatever things you ask when you pray, believe that you receive them, and you will have them."
>
> —MARK 11:22–24

> And whatever you ask in My name, that I will do, that the Father may be glorified in the Son. If you ask anything in My name, I will do it.
>
> —JOHN 14:13–14

This passage gives us one of the greatest lessons about prayer. Why are our prayers "in the name of Jesus" answered? "That the Father may be glorified in the Son." This is a fact we must never forget.

THE POWER OF THE SPOKEN WORD

One of the most overlooked sources of victory is the power of the spoken word. The world was created because "God said." Ten times in Genesis 1:1–29, the words, "God said" are recorded, and whatever He said happened the way He said. He did not struggle. He spoke the Word, and His spoken word was creative.

The same power was evident in the life and ministry of Jesus. A centurion (army officer who commanded one hundred soldiers) wanted his servant to be healed. He came to Jesus with these "faith words":

> "Lord, I am not worthy that You should come under my roof. But only speak a word, and my servant will be healed"...Then Jesus said to the centurion, "Go your way; and as you have believed, so let it be done for you." And his servant was healed that same hour.
>
> —MATTHEW 8:8, 13

This same creative word is available to us. Paul gives this revelation to the believers of the church:

"The word is near you, in your mouth and in your heart" (that is, the word of faith which we preach): that if you confess with your mouth the Lord Jesus and believe in your heart that God has raised Him from the dead, you will be saved. For with the heart one believes unto righteousness, and with the mouth confession is made unto salvation.

—ROMANS 10:8–10

- The word *saved* is the Greek *sozo* ("sode'-zo"), meaning "to save, deliver, protect, heal, preserve, do well and make whole, setting everything right."

- The word *salvation* is the Greek *soteria* ("so-tay-ree'-ah"), meaning "rescue, bring to safety, deliver, health and total salvation."

All of these provisions—physical, natural, and spiritual—come to us by believing in our hearts and confessing with our mouths. We do not confess our weaknesses. We confess the truth of God's Word. Real faith is saying what God says! If we will keep on confessing God's Word with our mouth, the spoken word of faith will overrule any unbelief and negative thoughts.

THE FINAL WORD ON SPIRITUAL WARFARE

The final word on spiritual warfare is found in the Bible and in the example of the Lord Jesus Christ. The most important scripture dealing with our warfare against Satan is found in James 4:7, "Therefore submit to God. Resist the devil and he will flee from you."

After Jesus had fasted for forty days, the devil came against Him with three temptations (Matthew 4; Luke 4), and Jesus, the Son of God, defeated him. However, Jesus did not use "God power" to defeat the devil. He used "Word power." Three times Satan came against Jesus, and each time He said, "It is written!" Each time He resisted the devil by quoting the Word of God to him. When we know God and have faith in Him and His Word, we can "resist the devil and he will flee from [us]" (James 4:7). God's Word in our hearts and in our mouths is a powerful weapon. This is the way we do spiritual warfare. This is the way we defeat the devil.

Instructions for Successful Praying

1. First, some miscellaneous advice about stopping occasionally to listen.

    A. Keep a notebook or recorder handy. When you hear something from God, do not let the devil steal it out of your heart.

    B. He may say something about contacting others and making things right. Whatever He says to you, do it!

    C. He may cause you to stop for a moment, read from the Scriptures, and receive new spiritual insight.

2. When you cannot pray for an hour, do not let that stop you from praying at all.

I teach our people the power of a five-minute prayer. Do each of these things for one minute:

    A. *Praise God* for who He is and for your salvation, family, and health.

    B. *Confess your faults and sins,* for you and your family. Ask forgiveness, for God has promised to forgive when we confess (1 John 1:9).

    C. *Pray for the church*—its leaders and all its ministries.

    D. *Pray for conditions and problems*—yours and those of your family, the church, and society (concerns such as crime, drugs, abortion, and poverty).

    E. *Pray for the harvest—local and worldwide.* Pray for missionaries and nations and their capital cities.

Examples of Powerful Short Prayers

While we are on the subject of short prayers, remember these events:

    1. *Elijah* prayed sixty-three words; the fire fell, turning a nation back to God (1 Kings 18:36–37).

2. *Hezekiah* prayed thirty words and saved his life (2 Kings 20:3).

3. *The publican* prayed seven words, and God heard him (Luke 18:13).

4. *The thief on the cross* prayed nine words and entered into paradise (Luke 23:42).

5. *The early church* had an emergency in Acts 4:24–31. The prayers of Peter and John and others lasted less than one minute:

When they prayed, the place where they were assembled together was shaken; they were all filled with the Holy Spirit, and they spoke the word of God with boldness.

—ACTS 4:31

WHAT CAN HINDER OUR PRAYERS FROM BEING ANSWERED?

After serving as pastor of one church for most of my adult life, I have observed a pattern of four basic problems that will keep our prayers from being answered:

1. Unconfessed sin: You know it is there, and it hinders your faith. Psalm 66:18 says, "If I regard iniquity in my heart, the Lord will not hear."

2. Wrong motives: James 4:3 says, "You ask and do not receive, because you ask amiss, that you may spend it on your pleasures."

3. An unforgiving spirit: Mark 11:25–26 says, "And whenever you stand praying, if you have anything against anyone, forgive him, that your Father in heaven may also forgive you your trespasses. But if you do not forgive, neither will your Father in heaven forgive your trespasses."

4. Lack of proper relationship with Jesus and His Word: John 15:7 says, "If you abide in Me, and My words abide in you, you will ask what you desire, and it shall be done for you." If

we do not abide in Him, and if we do not saturate ourselves with His Word, we can be sure our problems will abide.

PART II: PRAISE AND WORSHIP

Many religious people make a drastic mistake in either ignoring or rejecting praise and worship in their personal lives and in the activities of the church. They often feel it is something to do quickly so we can get to the message. However, one of the greatest tools of victory in the new covenant church is praise and worship. Why? It is the desire of God! He tells us in Psalm 50:23, "Whoever offers praise glorifies Me."

The basic revelation of the Bible is that God wants a people who will not only pray, but also praise and worship Him. The apostle Peter gives us this description of the New Testament (covenant) church:

> But you are a chosen generation, a royal priesthood, a holy nation, His own special people, that you may proclaim the praises of Him who called you out of darkness into His marvelous light.
> —1 PETER 2:9

The following statements will introduce the idea of praise. This theme is developed even more in my notes, called "The Pathway of Praise," in the *Spirit-Filled Life Bible.*[1]

THE EXAMPLE OF PRAISE IN THE OLD COVENANT

1. God inhabited (lived in) the praises of His people:

> But You are holy, enthroned in the praises of Israel. Our fathers trusted in You; they trusted, and You delivered them.
> —PSALM 22:3–4

The Hebrew word translated "enthroned" carries this meaning: "God sits down and makes Himself at home among us, dwells, abides, inhabits and continues with us." With this "praise attitude," the people of God "trusted" God, and He delivered them! He will do the same for us.

2. When any wickedness or attack came against them, they had the answer:

Behold, the wicked brings forth iniquity; yes, he conceives trouble and brings forth falsehood...I will praise the Lord according to His righteousness, and will sing praise to the name of the Lord Most High.

—PSALM 7:14, 17

3. The people of Israel knew they were pleasing and glorifying God in their praise:

Whoever offers praise glorifies Me; and to him who orders his conduct aright, I will show the salvation of God.

—PSALM 50:23

4. Israel learned that it is wise to praise God. To have His lovingkindness is the way to live. In fact, if we have life and breath, we are to praise God:

Because Your lovingkindness is better than life, My lips shall praise You. Thus I will bless You while I live; I will lift up my hands in Your name.

—PSALM 63:3–4

Let everything that has breath praise the Lord.

—PSALM 150:6

5. In Isaiah 61:3, we learn that "the garment of praise... [will take away] the spirit of heaviness." We all know the feeling of despair, depression, and hopelessness. The cure for all of these is to live in an atmosphere of praise.

THE EXAMPLE OF PRAISE IN THE NEW COVENANT CHURCH

1. One of the great revelations about the power of praise begins in Psalm 8:1–2:

O Lord, our Lord, How excellent is Your name in all the earth, Who have set Your glory above the heavens! Out of the mouth of babes and nursing infants You have ordained strength.

This prophetic word is fulfilled in the life of Jesus in Matthew 21:14–16:

> Then the blind and the lame came to Him in the temple, and He healed them. But when the chief priests and scribes saw the wonderful things that He did, and the children crying out in the temple and saying, "Hosanna to the Son of David!" they were indignant and said to Him, "Do You hear what these are saying?" And Jesus said to them, "Yes. Have you never read, 'Out of the mouth of babes and nursing infants You have perfected praise'?" [See also Psalm 8:2.]

Notice the word *strength* in Psalm 8. In Matthew 21, Jesus reveals what produces this strength, and it is praise.

2. When we come together in worship, we can strengthen and encourage each other with our songs and spiritual praise. In today's church world, many people only sing the latest choruses. We do not want to leave anyone behind, so I encourage worship leaders to present a balance to the people—"psalms and hymns [old and new] and spiritual songs":

> And do not be drunk with wine, in which is dissipation; but be filled with the Spirit, speaking to one another in psalms and hymns and spiritual songs, singing and making melody in your heart to the Lord.
> —EPHESIANS 5:18–19

3. Jesus is so closely identified with His people, His family, that when they sing praise in the house of God, Jesus is singing praise with them:

> For both He who sanctifies and those who are being sanctified are all of one, for which reason He is not ashamed to call them brethren, saying:

> "I will declare Your name to My brethren; in the midst of the assembly I will sing praise to You."
> —HEBREWS 2:11–12

4. Praise is not just in our minds. It is an audible "sacrifice ... to

God." Hebrews 13:15 says, "Therefore by Him let us continually offer the sacrifice of praise to God, that is, the fruit of our lips, giving thanks to His name."

5. The Bible says we are "kings and priests" to God (Rev. 1:6; 5:10). The apostle Peter explains how this priestly ministry works. Remember, he is describing the church:

But you are a chosen generation, a royal priesthood, a holy nation, His own special people, that you may proclaim the praises of Him who called you out of darkness into His marvelous light.

—1 PETER 2:9

DEFINING THE TERMS *PRAISE* AND *WORSHIP*

We deal with praise and worship together because they flow together so closely in the Bible. In the Old Testament, the Hebrew word for praise is *yadah* ("yaw-daw"), meaning "to hold out the hand, especially, to revere or worship with extended hands, to be thankful."

The New Testament has two main words. One is *ainos* ("ah'ee-nos"), meaning simply "praise of God." The main Greek word is *doxa* ("dox'-ah"), meaning "giving glory, dignity, honor, praise, and worship." This is where we get our word *doxology*—"the word of praise and worship." There is also the word *humneo* ("hoom-neh'-o"), meaning "a hymn, to sing, to celebrate God in song."

The Old Testament word for worship is *shachah* ("shaw-khaw"), meaning "to prostrate, especially in paying respect to God, to bow down, humbly beseech, make obeisance, do reverence and worship." The New Testament word for worship is *proskuneo* ("pros-koo-neh'-o"), meaning "to kiss the hand, prostrate oneself in homage, reverence and adoration."

This scripture sets the tone for worship:

Give to the Lord the glory due His name; bring an offering, and come before Him. Oh, worship the Lord in the beauty of holiness!

—1 CHRONICLES 16:29

When Joshua worshiped, God gave him the plan to take the city of Jericho:

231

And it came to pass, when Joshua was by Jericho, that he lifted his eyes and looked, and behold, a Man stood opposite him with His sword drawn in His hand. And Joshua went to Him and said to Him, "Are You for us or for our adversaries?" So He said, "No, but as Commander of the army of the Lord I have now come." And Joshua fell on his face to the earth and worshiped, and said to Him, "What does my Lord say to His servant?" Then the Commander of the Lord's army said to Joshua, "Take your sandal off your foot, for the place where you stand is holy." And Joshua did so.

—JOSHUA 5:13–15

Now Jericho was securely shut up because of the children of Israel; none went out, and none came in. And the Lord said to Joshua: "See! I have given Jericho into your hand, its king, and the mighty men of valor."

—JOSHUA 6:1–2

God commanded Israel many times that it should not worship idols. We are commanded not to bow down and worship anything we create:

Your carved images I will also cut off, and your sacred pillars from your midst; you shall no more worship the work of your hands.

—MICAH 5:13

WE LEARN MANY TRUTHS ABOUT WORSHIP IN THE NEW TESTAMENT

- The wise men came to see Jesus. They did not worship the star, but Him:

Where is He who has been born King of the Jews? For we have seen His star in the East and have come to worship Him.

—MATTHEW 2:2

- In His contest with the devil, Jesus says we shall worship no one but God. We are not to worship or adore any apostle, any angel, nor Mary:

Then Jesus said to him, "Away with you, Satan! For it is written, 'You shall worship the Lord your God, and Him only you shall serve.'"

—MATTHEW 4:10

- God the Father emphatically states that Jesus is to be worshiped:

For to which of the angels did He ever say: "You are My Son, today I have begotten You"? And again: "I will be to Him a Father, and He shall be to Me a Son"? But when He again brings the firstborn into the world, He says: "Let all the angels of God worship Him."

—HEBREWS 1:5–6

- When we worship, great victories of deliverance will be won:

Now when they began to sing and to praise, the Lord set ambushes against the people of Ammon, Moab, and Mount Seir, who had come against Judah; and they were defeated.

—2 CHRONICLES 20:22

But at midnight Paul and Silas were praying and singing hymns to God, and the prisoners were listening to them. Suddenly there was a great earthquake, so that the foundations of the prison were shaken; and immediately all the doors were opened and everyone's chains were loosed.

—ACTS 16:25–26

Finally, let me encourage everyone: do not give in to any negative feeling. All of us eventually walk in a "dry" place where we struggle with our circumstances. We can be defeated, or we can gain a great victory. I love the Bible story where Israel came to a dry well, and "the Lord said to Moses, 'Gather the people together, and I will give them water.' Then Israel sang this song: 'Spring up, O well! All of you sing to it'" (Num. 21:16–17). The waters began to flow.

As you read these final words, make plans to get alone with God. Enter into His presence with thanksgiving, praise, and worship. Build up your faith; begin to pray and communicate with God. Then stop and listen. He will answer!

NOTES

Chapter 11
Jesus: His Humiliation and Exaltation
1. William R. Newell and Daniel B. Towner, "At Calvary," 1895. Public Domain.

Chapter 17
Resurrection and Eternal Judgment
1. Ralph Wilkerson, *Beyond and Back* (New York: Bantam Books, 1978).

Chapter 22
Prayer, Praise, and Worship
1. Jack Hayford, ed., *Spirit-Filled Life Bible* (Nashville, TN: Thomas Nelson Publishers, 1991).

AUTHOR'S NOTE

I first taught this material to a class of two hundred people. Some were new Christians; others were leaders in our Faith Church in New Orleans, Louisiana. Scores of them expressed their appreciation in written notes, saying it was the most interesting and exciting class they had ever taken.

If this book is to be taught to a class of students, we have extra teaching notes and a Questions and Answers booklet available.

I would like to hear from you after you have finished this book. Your comments would be greatly appreciated.

Charles Green

13123 I–10 Service Road
New Orleans, LA 70128

www.HarvestMinistriesOnLine.com